"In *Overcoming Fear*, and deliverance. She sk truth that for me were very liberating. She further …… to deeper revelation with activation prayers and declarations. I found the text to be thoroughly delightful and challenging. *Overcoming Fear* is a must-read!"

Norman Benz, D.Min., lead pastor, Covenant Centre International; co-founder, Renewing South Florida

"Dawna De Silva's recipe for overcoming fear has been tested by thousands of people, and it works. You will not be disappointed if you try it. Your victory over fear is within these pages."

Faith Blatchford, author, *Winning the Battle for the Night: God's Plan for Sleep, Dreams and Revelation*

"Few women on the planet are as qualified to talk about over-coming fear as Dawna De Silva. Dawna has spent a lifetime helping to discover, master and equip others in a lifestyle of freedom. In *Overcoming Fear*, you'll learn through her practical and biblical approach all the necessary ingredients you need to get and stay free. Read this book!"

Havilah Cunnington, founder, Truth to Table; author, *Stronger Than the Struggle*

"*Overcoming Fear* is a practical manual on not just getting free of fear, but staying free of fear. I would trust Dawna with my life and listen carefully to her instruction for freedom because she has proven to be one who can lead you there. Get ready to be empowered and walk out new levels of personal freedom as you stir up the ingredients of a fear-free life."

Randy Hill, senior leader, Summit Church; author, *Encounters: Stories of Healing* and *PK and the Guardians of the Heart*

"Dawna partners with the Holy Spirit to pull out rooted lies from the garden of your heart. I remember the first time I heard her message on overcoming fear. It had such clarity and power. I cannot recommend this teaching or this person more highly. Do yourself a favor and read this book. Who knows how much spiritual baggage you will lose!"

Jenn Johnson, Bethel Music

"I heard Dawna speak this message on overcoming fear using this wonderful recipe metaphor and was deeply impacted by her words—so much so that I remember her sermon almost verbatim. It's in my top five messages I've heard in my Christian life. This book is that message."

Don Potter, Potterhaus Music and Potter School Haus;
singer/songwriter, producer and musician;
author, *Facing the Wall*, *The Things I Thought I Knew*
and *John: A Layman's Look at the Disciple Jesus Loved*

"Your unconquered fears are the greatest hindrance to fulfilling your destiny. This world is full of people paralyzed with fear. Dawna isn't. She is bold as a lion. *Overcoming Fear* is full of practical yet supernatural ingredients and relatable stories that will free you to unlock your full potential."

Duncan and Kate Smith, presidents, Catch the Fire

"Dawna De Silva has powerfully put together a recipe of success for combating fear. She has gracefully provided key ingredients in order to create a healthy lifestyle of love through the application of God's truths. Dawna provides revelation that frees and delivers you from fear as you read!"

Beatriz Zaldana, founder, Convergence Ministry

Overcoming
FEAR

Overcoming
FEAR

THE SUPERNATURAL STRATEGY TO LIVE IN FREEDOM

DAWNA DE SILVA

Chosen

a division of Baker Publishing Group
Minneapolis, Minnesota

Published by Chosen Books
11400 Hampshire Avenue South
Bloomington, Minnesota 55438
www.chosenbooks.com

Chosen Books is a division of
Baker Publishing Group, Grand Rapids, Michigan

Printed in the United States of America

ISBN 978-0-8007-9920-5

Library of Congress Cataloging-in-Publication Control Number: 2018053591

The stories in this book, while faithfully representing each account of a person's freedom, have been modified to protect the person's identity. Otherwise, they represent real people in real situations.

Cover design by Rob Williams, InsideOutCreativeArts

19 20 21 22 23 24 25   7 6 5 4 3 2 1

This book is dedicated
to my heroes—
all who have won their battles
against fear.

Contents

Contents

Foreword

L ove and fear are mortal enemies. They displace one another, similar to the dynamic of light and darkness. These foes cannot occupy the same space. When we allow fear to become our counselor, we invite the destructive enemy of love. The Bible says:

> There is no fear in love [dread does not exist], but full-grown (complete, perfect) love turns fear out of doors and expels every trace of terror! For fear brings with it the thought of punishment, and [so] he who is afraid has not reached the full maturity of love [is not yet grown into love's complete perfection].
>
> 1 John 4:18 AMPC, emphasis added

Simply put, we must learn to use the voice of love as our counselor in relationships and other daily situations.

The keys to freedom are simple, but it takes training and courage to hold onto the breakthroughs that they bring. Only the bravest people can lead us into new places of freedom. Dawna De Silva is one of these people.

In these pages, Dawna will show you how to use biblical keys to break free from the strains of fear. In *Overcoming Fear: The*

Supernatural Strategy to Live in Freedom, Dawna's practical style shines forth. As we all know, truth is what ultimately sets us free, and Dawna takes plenty of time to pack truth into her book.

In all my years of pastoring, I have never met a single person who is totally free. I have, however, seen many people who are less afraid than I. These people shrug off fear of failure, disregard anxieties based in rejection and charge forward in the face of uncertainty. Their "fear-less" levels are connected to their experiences with God that bring unlimited freedom.

Over the years, I have seen hundreds of people delivered from fear after spending time with Dawna and her team. It has become a launching point for many around the world. "Have you received a Sozo yet?" is a question I hear posed almost daily.

The everyday practice of knowing God, hearing Him and living in His Word is what chases fear away. I hope that you will increase in these tactics as you work through Dawna's book—and experience the same level of freedom people are having all across the globe.

These words are my hearty *amen* to Dawna's message. I have no doubt that you will find an effective recipe for fearless living in these pages. Congratulations. You have started a wonderful journey into an adventure with a loving God. I know how this story will end. You will become contagious with this freedom and will give it away to those around you. Your home, church and workplace will be filled with God's love as fear and darkness are displaced. Peace to your heart.

Blessings,
Danny Silk, president, Loving on Purpose Life Academy;
author, *Keep Your Love On* and *Powerful and Free*

Preface

Why the Recipe Metaphor?

I have always enjoyed metaphors. This is probably because my dad writes poetry and can paint pictures in my mind with his words. He has not yet made it big with his writing, but I have always marveled at his skill in turning unrelated images into works of art. I hope this book achieves even a small measure of his gift.

Maybe because of my dad's writings, the Lord speaks to me by planting pictures in my mind. In the midst of a tough session, God will often give me pictures that I can use to open a dialogue with my client. This process of discovery often leads to prayers of freedom.

The recipe metaphor came from a picture given to me during a session with a client named Helen. I was leading her through a prayer when I noticed an image pop above her head. In the picture, I saw a kitchen shelf with three ingredients: flour, sugar and oil. What these pictures came to mean ended up being the center of my fear-free teaching and the core message of this book.

The Lord shared with me the verse 2 Timothy 1:7, which includes some of the most popular words in the Bible: "For God has not given us a spirit of fear . . . but of power, love, and self-discipline" (NLT). The Lord told me the ingredients—flour, sugar and oil—were metaphors for power, love and self-discipline. He then informed me that my client had removed power (flour) from her kitchen shelf in order to appear loving to her husband. It was an amazing revelation that changed my perspective on inner healing and the life of my client.

Part of my job, as the founder and overseer of Bethel Sozo, is to help people break free from bonds that hold them back. Fear is one of the most common tactics of the enemy. The recipe metaphor works because it is simple. If we keep power, love and self-discipline stocked in our hearts, then a spirit of fear will not be able to hold onto our lives.

I developed this idea and it became one of my most popular sermons. The first time I shared it at Bethel, I brought up an armful of kitchen ingredients (flour, sugar and oil, among others) and demonstrated how balancing each ingredient within the recipe creates a pure and fragrant offering to the Lord. Years later, "Recipe for a Fear-Free Life" remains one of my most popular teachings.

There are, of course, other tools you can use to dismantle the enemy's hold. I celebrate any healthy Christian ministry you find that can help you break free from torment. This message, based on Scripture, is structured to present a simple path toward fear-free living. It uses examples I have seen throughout my career as an inner healing and deliverance minister, and will, I hope, bring you ideas and revelations for breakthrough.

Acknowledgments

As with any book, *Overcoming Fear* involved a handful of helpers. These include: Stephen De Silva, my husband and champion of 38 years whose shared revelations continue to shore up my messages; my son Cory, who served as my writing partner and project manager; Susan Anderson, my friend and traveling partner who encouraged me to keep typing on our travels; Dawn and Debbie, my interns, for reading my manuscript over and over; Dale, for her editing skills; and many others who are not mentioned here. Without all of your help, this book would never have happened.

Introduction

It was the fall of 1984. My husband and I were young believers attending a small church in Sacramento, California. We were finishing up our bachelor's degrees at a university and had connected well with some of our Christian neighbors. After a while, they began to invite us over to pray and spend evenings in worship. We were excited when the family asked us to join them at church where their fifteen-year-old rebellious daughter would receive a much-needed time of deliverance.

Full of faith, Stephen and I filled our car with her extended family and headed out for the Sunday morning service. During the sermon, elders agreed to pray deliverance over the teenager while we and the family got to enjoy the service. To this day, I am not sure what took place in the back room where they ministered to the daughter. I do know that throughout the service we kept hearing growls, shouts and demonic taunts like, "I hate God" and "You can't stop me!"

Embarrassed, I melted into my pew, telling God, "I will do anything for you *but* deliverance." Interestingly, only fourteen years later my friend Teresa Liebscher and I began the International Bethel Sozo Ministry—a deliverance and inner healing ministry birthed out of Bethel Church in Redding, California. I have loved being part of deliverance ministry for more than twenty years. In just a few decades, I went from hating the idea of performing deliverances to running them. God really has a sense of humor.

Sozo comes from a Greek word that means "saved, healed and delivered." In Sozo, we help people strengthen connections with each member of the Trinity (Father, Son and Holy Spirit). Using proven tools, we help people identify which lies they believe about themselves and/or God, then invite them to replace any lies with truth. Replacing lies with truth allows our clients to move past deceptions so they can break free from sinful patterns developed over years of practice.[1]

Jesus' mission was to bring abundant life. We attain this gift by opening our hearts to the Lord's immeasurable love. There may be hurts or wounds in our lives, but none of these comes from the Lord. "The thief comes only to steal and kill and destroy. I came that they may have life and have it abundantly" (John 10:10).

Abundantly means "present in great quantity, more than adequate, over sufficient, [and] richly supplied, as with resources."[2] If any of these "richly supplied" experiences are absent in your life, you may want to spend time with God and allow Him to remove any lies or obstacles blocking His abundant life being manifested through you.

Overcoming Fear: The Supernatural Strategy to Live in Freedom came from my desire to help God's people reach their promised land. Too many Christians allow obstacles like fear to rule their lives when God's desire is for them to live courageously. My hope is that this book will help Christians stand victoriously over the devil's schemes.

My goal is to help you identify fears, patterns and lies that harm your connection with God and others. I will give you proven biblical tactics so you can stand above demonic attacks and break free from oppression. The focus of this book is fear, but other issues (like bitterness, lies, lack of boundaries and addictions) will also be discussed. By the end of this book, you should be able to recognize self-protective patterns in your life and learn how you can surrender them to God and live powerfully.

If this book does nothing more than introduce you to a more personal relationship with Jesus, I will consider it a success. He is the only true solution for anyone who wants to walk in freedom. I pray these pages provide a fun, insightful read, and above all, that you will learn how to replace fear with God's truth. Let the road to fearless living begin.

Fear

Anxiety in a man's heart weighs him down, but a
good word makes him glad.

Proverbs 12:25

1

The Problem with Fear

A shrill scream shot from the living room. "Mom!" I stumbled out of bed and into the hallway. My two-year-old son was chasing after his older brother with a knife in his hands. Registering the danger, I leapt forward, yelling, "Put that knife down!"

To this day, I have no idea why my son was chasing his brother or what even happened after he dropped the knife. I am sure it involved my giving some strong explanations like, "You can't just pick up a knife and start chasing people," but it imprinted on me a near-traumatic experience. What if my son had actually stabbed him?

Every parent has shouted at a child racing toward a busy street or heading straight for danger. Throughout my parental career, a raised voice seemed like a successful parenting tool. At times, shouting became a technique I could use to protect and train my children.

An office center where I once worked was not well lit at night. Everyone left early, so it often fell to me to lock up and make the long trek through the parking lot.

One night I had a sense someone was watching me, so I switched off the lights in my office and peeked out. I waited a few minutes and saw nothing. I turned the lights back on and resumed my work but could not shake this feeling of being watched. Two hours later, I finally called it a night, locked up the main doors and headed outside.

Crossing the lot, I felt a sudden urge to raise my shirt collar to protect my throat. I thought, *I hope there aren't any vampires out tonight.*

Thinking about this, I stopped several feet from my car and laughed.

What am I doing? I thought. *Vampires? This is so irrational!*

The next day, I attended a meeting with the building's security advisor. When he asked me how I was doing, I recounted laughingly the previous night's occurrence.

The security advisor asked, "Dawna, what time was that?"

"9:40 p.m.," I said, intrigued.

"Last night," he said, "I had my first-ever panic attack, and it started right at 9:40. My wife had to coax me out of a fetal position so I could get off the floor. I kept trying to tell myself, 'This is so irrational.'"

We discussed this and sank back in silence. Though it manifested differently for each of us, we had both partnered with the enemy's broadcast of irrational fear.

About six years ago, my family went on a hike through Palos Verdes in Southern California. It led us to a high cliff beside the sea that dropped about five hundred feet. Though it was steep, I was able to hold onto branches, rocks and roots to get down until we made it to a path that wandered along the coastal wall. With the tide coming in and fearing we would not have time to retrace our steps, we decided to head back up a different path.

Halfway up, I made the unfortunate mistake of looking down. The sea roared below, and a sense of dread shook my body. Until that moment, I had no idea how steep this cliff was.

What are you doing? my mind shouted. *One slip and you're gone!*

My heart screamed. Using a helpful Sozo tool (*Presenting Jesus*), I asked, "Jesus, where are You right now?"

I felt His peace come over me, and I finally resumed my climb. I rounded a jagged boulder and found my seventeen-year-old son, Tim, huddled against the rocks. Reaching out, he said, "Mom, be careful. It's steep. Take my hand and I can help you reach the top."

Instantly, an image came to mind—*I took my son's hand and we slipped. Both of us tumbled to the waves below.*

I did not reach for his hand. I froze.

"Mom?"

Tim knelt beside me as I hugged the rocks. A smile creased his face, but I felt safety slipping further and further away.

"I'm just kidding, Mom. It's not that steep."

"Just go," I said, shaking. "I'll meet you there."

Tim stood, easily climbing the rest of the way. I gathered the last of my strength and pushed myself up the path. When I finally reached the summit, I latched onto the nearest fence, shook uncontrollably and wept.

After experiencing this event, I can understand how people encounter such overwhelming fear that it paralyzes their bodies and erases all common sense. Thankfully, this was only a one-time occurrence for me.

No Fear

We serve a triune God and are made in His image (see Genesis 1:27). It should not surprise us, then, to find an interesting likeness: He is three Persons (see Luke 3:22); and we, too, are of tripartite design (see 1 Thessalonians 5:23). Each of the previous examples shows how fear affects the human soul (mind, will and emotions), body (physical sensations) and spirit (picking up fear from the spiritual realm).

Studies show that anxiety has negative consequences on the human body. Not only does it weaken our immune systems, accelerate aging and muddy our senses, in some cases, it can even cause death.[1] This is not to say that all physical or emotional torment is linked to fear, but it does show how the condition of the soul and spirit affects our bodies.

Paul told the Philippians, "Do not be anxious about anything" (Philippians 4:6). Jesus commanded His disciples not to worry (see Matthew 6:34). God commanded Joshua and the Israelites to be strong and very courageous (see Joshua 1:7). The Bible's repeated commands to "fear not" reinforce our calling as powerful champions in God's Kingdom. Our Lord is the good and perfect Father. As His children, we must follow His example and live a life free from fear. "There is no fear in love, but perfect love casts out fear. For fear has to do with punishment, and whoever fears has not been perfected in love" (1 John 4:18).

Situations may arise where not experiencing fear seems impossible, but we must remember that living with fear is a choice—not a consequence of human life. "Fear not, for I am with you; be not dismayed, for I am your God; I will strengthen you, I will help you, I will uphold you with my righteous right hand" (Isaiah 41:10).

Faith in God should be our spiritual default. Successful fear-free living comes when we partner with God's goodness and reject the enemy's influence of fear.

In Joshua, twelve spies saw the Promised Land, yet only two brought back a hopeful report. The spies who brought back a fearful report convinced the Israelites to delay going into the Promised Land. Like the ten spies, many of us focus on what is lacking rather than searching for the promises of God. This poor focus leads to stress, anxiety and, in some cases, physical consequences.

God desires to see us grow, so He allows us to encounter situations where we may feel less than comfortable. These are not meant to be seasons of defeat. They are meant to inspire and encourage us to get past the obstacles that have been holding us back. When we find ourselves in periods of growth, fear can be a constant voice hounding us. Those who master fear-free living have the strength to reject the enemy's voice.

God's command to "fear not" appears constantly throughout Scripture. Pastor Rick Warren, among others, states that this is intentional, and that fear-free living is simply a heavenly concept that all believers should follow.

> Why did God stress the importance of avoiding fear? Because our hurts and hang-ups can often cause us to think that God is out to get us, that all He wants to do is condemn us and punish us. But that simply isn't true. Jesus is proof of that. When Christians form a healthy relationship with God and understand His eternal grace and mercy, they will realize that there is no real need for fear.[2]

Fear is not God's way of punishing us. It is simply the enemy's attempt to persuade us to focus on what is lacking rather than the Lord's abundance.

Years ago my friend Pat, a retired police officer, was enlisted to help train other police officers in Iraq. Even though the war was winding down, there were still daily bouts of violence throughout the country. Pat told me that every morning at daybreak he would go up to the roof of his apartment building and worship God.

When he told me this, I said, "Pat, weren't you scared?"

"No," he said. "I knew I was where God wanted me to be, so I decided to look for His presence wherever I was to release

Him into my circumstances. I realized that fear was a belief that at any time something bad could happen. I decided to worship God with the expectation that something good would happen instead."

Pat's response was poignant. It revealed how the devil often exploits our fears so that we focus on expected harm rather than God's protection. The success of our ability to thrive in fearful situations is in resisting the devil's taunts so we can embrace faith instead of fear. If the devil can keep us in a constant state of questioning the Lord's commands or goodness, our white flags of surrender will easily and quickly unfurl.

This is how it was with the Israelites when the twelve spies returned from the Promised Land to give their reports. Only two saw God's provision, while ten focused on the giants. The fearful report swayed God's people not to enter their Promised Land, causing a forty-year wilderness journey. So it can be with believers who stop short of abundant life because of fear, discouragement or hopelessness.

Scripture As a Weapon

Achieving a fear-free lifestyle takes work. Meditating on God's truth is a helpful way to focus on God's promises rather than the enemy's attacks. I encourage you to find Scriptures that will strengthen your resolve to stand against the enemy. Memorize verses and speak them out loud throughout your day. God's Word is mighty for the tearing down of strongholds. Here are some powerful examples to help you get started.

Against Discouragement and Hopelessness

Arise, shine, for your light has come, and the glory of the Lord has risen upon you. For behold, darkness shall cover the earth, and thick darkness the peoples; but the Lord will arise upon

you, and his glory will be seen upon you. And nations shall
come to your light, and kings to the brightness of your rising.

Isaiah 60:1–3

For Provisional Needs

"The LORD will open to you his good treasury, the heavens, to
give the rain to your land in its season and to bless all the work
of your hands. And you shall lend to many nations, but you shall
not borrow. And the LORD will make you the head and not the
tail, and you shall only go up and not down, if you obey the
commandments of the LORD your God, which I command you
today, being careful to do them."

Deuteronomy 28:12–13

"And why are you anxious about clothing? Consider the lilies
of the field, how they grow: they neither toil nor spin, yet I
tell you, even Solomon in all his glory was not arrayed like
one of these."

Matthew 6:28–29

When Facing a Possible Life Change

"Be strong and courageous, for you shall cause this people to
inherit the land that I swore to their fathers to give them. Only
be strong and very courageous, being careful to do according
to all the law that Moses my servant commanded you. Do not
turn from it to the right hand or to the left, that you may have
good success wherever you go."

Joshua 1:6–7

If Feeling Life Is Out of Control

"And which of you by being anxious can add a single hour to
his span of life?"

Matthew 6:27

Jesus Himself was in the stern, asleep on the cushion; and they woke Him and said to Him, "Teacher, do You not care that we are perishing?" And He got up and rebuked the wind and said to the sea, "Hush, be still." And the wind died down and it became perfectly calm.

Mark 4:38–39 NASB

After reading through these verses, allow the Holy Spirit to reveal His truth about your current situation. If you are battling other issues that are not listed above, ask God to show you some verses that correspond to your season. God's Word is the foundation for combating fear. Choose a verse and ponder it today.

GROUP DISCUSSION QUESTIONS

1. Do you identify with any of the examples of fear listed in this chapter?
2. If so, which story caught your attention and why?
3. Do you find yourself focusing more on what you already have or what you currently lack?
4. Do you constantly battle being afraid or would you consider yourself to be generally fear-free?

ACTIVATION PRAYERS

1. Ask the Holy Spirit to show you any fear you are currently dealing with.
2. Ask Him if there is a lie you are believing that is empowering this fear.
3. Ask Him where you learned this lie. (Was it during childhood? Who taught it to you?)

4. Forgive anyone who taught you that this lie was truth.

5. Hand the lie to Jesus and ask Him what truth He wants to give you in its place.

6. Ask Him to give you a practical tool, step or plan for combating the fear.

DECLARATIONS

1. I am a child of the King of kings (see Romans 8:15).

2. I am seen and protected by my Father in heaven (see Psalm 91).

3. God is my light and my salvation; I will not be afraid (see Psalm 27:1).

2

The Recipe Revealed

For God has not given us a spirit of fear, but of power and of love and of a sound mind.

2 Timothy 1:7 NKJV

Helen, the wife of a busy entrepreneur, sat in my office. She had married a year earlier, but her first twelve months with her husband had been anything but blissful. She told me the atmosphere in her home was tense, and the slightest disagreement with her husband ended up triggering her into heated moments of rage. Helen knew she had a problem; she just could not figure out how to fix it.

Beginning our session, I asked, "Holy Spirit, is there anything You want Helen to know?"

Instantly, I saw a picture. In it was a kitchen shelf. On the shelf were three ingredients: flour, sugar and oil. I heard the Lord say these represented power, love and self-discipline—the same ones listed in Paul's famous passage to Timothy. In the picture, Helen's hand reached up and removed flour and oil from the shelf. Only sugar remained.

I asked Helen, "Where did you learn that power and love could not exist in the same recipe?"

Stunned by the question, she took a few seconds to respond.

"From my parents. I think."

Helen went on to confess that her parents had always taught her to be "loving" no matter what. This loving attitude tended to manifest itself in the action of remaining silent. When people mistreated her, she was told to "turn the other cheek" and avoid confrontation. Making people feel "loved" was her family's top priority.

As Helen entered into adulthood, her brother began using drugs. No communication with the intent to help him was happening, so she asked her parents, "Why aren't you guys doing anything? Why are we allowing him to implode our family with dysfunction, thievery and angry outbursts?"

Her parents' reply was, "We know he's struggling, dear, but we just need to be loving."

This went on for years.. Helen embraced the silence until it became so suffocating that she would erupt into bouts of rage. Unintentionally, she began to spice her arguments with tantrums that seemed to amplify her voice. As she grew, this became a pattern of communication in her family.

Now, as a newly married woman trying to be loving, Helen found herself falling back into a cycle of powerless silence. Deep down, she wanted to express love for her spouse, but her tool kit only allowed for silent acceptance as a sign of love. By not having proper communication skills, she allowed her power to be removed.

Unfortunately, like Helen, when our recipes are out of order, we choose alternate ingredients to add to our recipes to try to balance them out. But rarely does this ever work (at least in a healthy way).

Recipe for Combating Fear

This encounter with Helen reinforced the truth that God has a recipe for combating fear. Its formula is simple: power + love + self-discipline (see 2 Timothy 1:7 NLT). If we balance these ingredients equally, there is no tactic the devil can use to trick us into partnering with fear. In Helen's case, the devil's tactic was a lie that said, *Helen, if you don't use rage to amplify your voice, nobody will listen to you.* Fortunately, as the Holy Spirit revealed truth, Helen was able to break free from the lie and her partnership with rage.

When our formulas are out of balance, fear takes control of our lives. I find that most of our struggles can be boiled down to fear—like the fear of being harmed, or the fear of not having enough, or the fear of being overlooked or forgotten. I believe this is why God gives us daily doses of truth in His Word. He knows that unless we have access to His truth, the enemy's lies of fear will overwhelm us.

Throughout my day, I encounter people wrestling with fear in many different ways. Sometimes just looking at someone can tell me if that person is struggling with fear. But many times we do not discern the fear others are carrying until an inappropriate behavior pops out. This was a lesson I learned personally while on a trip home.

When my Sozo team and I arrived at the airport, we were assaulted with an overwhelming atmosphere of fear. We headed toward our airline check-in to find that nearly all the flights from Paris had been either delayed or cancelled. We decided to search for food in case our delay would be long. To our surprise, we found that almost all the food and water bottles in the airport had been purchased. I could actually feel myself starting to think, *Oh no! How will we find food for ourselves?* I had to remind myself that all of Paris could not be out of food. This was an internal battle to overcome my fear of lack.

As we returned to our check-in counter (nearly empty-handed), a group of travelers began shouting at the clerk running the check-in desk beside ours. Their inner battle against inconvenience and the fear of not reaching their destination on time was manifesting physically. As the crowd grew, it seemed as if a full-blown riot would break out. The authorities even had to remove people from the airport. All this continued to increase the tension in the area and, honestly, even our team had to take thoughts of fear captive while releasing peace to those around us.

The frenzy we encountered in the airport reminds me of a story in the Bible:

> On that day, when evening had come, he said to them, "Let us go across to the other side." And leaving the crowd, they took him with them in the boat, just as he was. And other boats were with him. And a great windstorm arose, and the waves were breaking into the boat, so that the boat was already filling. But he was in the stern, asleep on the cushion. And they woke him and said to him, "Teacher, do you not care that we are perishing?" And he awoke and rebuked the wind and said to the sea, "Peace! Be still!" And the wind ceased, and there was a great calm.
>
> Mark 4:35–39

I can identify with the rising panic the disciples felt as the winds tossed their boat to and fro, as well as the sense of being out of control and at the mercy of their surroundings. Jesus, however, was undisturbed by the outside forces. His ability to not be moved by fear equipped Him with power to introduce peace into the situation. The result was an astonished crew marveling at how even the winds and waves obeyed Him.

According to studies, almost half of all working adults in America suffer from anxiety. In addition, up to forty percent of adults suffer from severe disorders like phobias or panic attacks.[1] This shows how many people in the world are stressed and in need of God's fear-free strategy.

Finding this strategy is what Helen and I worked on during our session. I led her through forgiveness—first with her brother for his lies and for causing constant turmoil in the family. I then had her forgive her parents for failing to build strong boundaries and for not engaging in brave communication. Finally, I had Helen ask God to forgive her for partnering with rage as a way to gain power in a seemingly powerless situation.

Like Helen, we, too, can work through our own inner healing processes so we can remove lies (spices/substitutes) that get in the way of fear-free living. If we ask the Holy Spirit for His perspective on our situations, He will give us insight as to how to balance our own formulas against fear.

If you struggle with fear in any area of your life (finances, relationships, failure . . .), take a moment to ask God what He thinks about your recipe. Picture your own personal kitchen shelf. Are power, love and self-discipline in proper balance, or are you allowing alternate spices like rage, pride or self-sufficiency to disrupt your peace?

Where Does Fear Come From?

Many theories exist on the origin of fear. For Christians, of course, the simple answer is to say—the devil. But there are different types of fear, and some are not as easily decipherable as others. Although I am not a huge fan of Sigmund Freud, I found this statement from him to be quite insightful:

> Real fear seems quite rational and comprehensible to us. We may testify that it is a reaction to the perception of external

danger, [that is] harm that is expected and foreseen. It is related to the flight reflex and may be regarded as an expression of the instinct of self-preservation.[2]

Research shows that as a response to survival, stress hormones like norepinephrine and cortisol can be released from the brain to flood your body and act like a chemical messenger that says, "Run!" I personally do not see this chemical response to fear as evil, but rather a biological safety valve God placed inside of us to keep us alive in harmful situations.

The type of fear I will focus on in this book is the fear that takes the place of our trusting in God. This is the fear that follows us home after a long day of work and keeps us awake at night. It is the fear that comes from the enemy's lies and draws our faith away from God's ability to provide and care for our needs. It is the fear that shouts at us to "look here" instead of at God's eternal promises.

This fear comes directly from the enemy and has no place in a Christian's life. We have no time to struggle with anxieties, doubts and worries. We have a world to reach and save! In the book of Matthew, Jesus tells His disciples not to worry about needs like food or provision. Instead, He encourages them to seek first the Kingdom of God and watch as all their needs are supplied (see 6:31–33). Fear of lack is an insult to the very care of God for you and your circumstances.

Sometimes fear develops in us from the unresolved wounds we carry from childhood. These wounds can be from traumatic events like abuse, harmful accidents or simple misunderstandings with others that get processed incorrectly in our hearts and minds. In Sozo, we call these unresolved hurts *father, sibling or mother wounds.*

It is vital in our process of learning how to combat fear that we ferret out the unhealthy mindsets we have carried into adulthood. These mindsets sabotage our ability to trust God in all our circumstances. It is why we are told in 2 Corinthians 10:5 to "demolish arguments and every pretension that sets itself up against the knowledge of God, and . . . take captive every thought to make it obedient to Christ" (NIV).

Origin of Lies

The needs of protection, provision and identity contribute to a person's overall sense of security. If one or more of these areas are left unaddressed or unmet, especially in childhood, our own perceptions start to take root. We begin to make assumptions about people and our world around us. Since we are judging the world by our own set of circumstances and through our own eyes, rarely do we come to a proper faith-filled conclusion.

My husband likens the origin of lies to seeds being dropped into the fertile soils of our hearts through our experiences. These seeds (lies) grow as we water. Every time we agree with or partner with a lie, we make it stronger. Eventually, if these lies are not dealt with, they will grow strong and influence our lives and actions. Dr. Caroline Leaf covers this idea in her book *Switch On Your Brain: The Key to Peak Happiness, Thinking, and Health.*[3] In it, she discusses the idea of "toxic thoughts" and how we can partner with God to dispel their influence.

An excellent resource for identifying and healing lies is a Sozo tool my friend Teresa and I call the *Father Ladder*. Using this tool, clients can examine their relationships with God (the Father, Son and Holy Spirit) and see if any lies are hindering their connection with Him. In the Sozo ministry, we find a correlation between each member of the Trinity and the specific needs they provide for us. We see how Father God meets our needs for identity, provision and protection, while Jesus satisfies our hunger for communication and companionship. Finally, we notice how the Holy Spirit provides our needs for comfort and instruction.

Each of these needs can be met and expressed in a healthy family unit. Though the Trinity is our ultimate source for meeting all of these needs, the family unit should be a representation of the Godhead here on earth, displaying godly characteristics. Here is some information illustrating this concept:

Father God

Earthly fathers, like our heavenly Father, are the ones who usually provide identity, provision and protection to the family.

Identity/Value

"Before I formed you in the womb I knew you, and before you were born I consecrated you; I appointed you a prophet to the nations."

Jeremiah 1:5

But you are a chosen race, a royal priesthood, a holy nation, a people for his own possession, that you may proclaim the excellencies of him who called you out of darkness into his marvelous light. Once you were not a people, but now you are God's people; once you had not received mercy, but now you have received mercy.

1 Peter 2:9–10

He was still speaking when, behold, a bright cloud overshadowed them, and a voice from the cloud said, "This is my beloved Son, with whom I am well pleased; listen to him."

Matthew 17:5

Protection

"Fear not, for I am with you; be not dismayed, for I am your God; I will strengthen you, I will help you, I will uphold you with my righteous right hand."

Isaiah 41:10

But the Lord is faithful. He will establish you and guard you against the evil one.

2 Thessalonians 3:3

Provision

The LORD does not let the righteous go hungry, but he thwarts the craving of the wicked.

Proverbs 10:3

"Look at the birds of the air: they neither sow nor reap nor gather into barns, and yet your heavenly Father feeds them. Are you not of more value than they?"

Matthew 6:26

"Or what man is there among you who, when his son asks for a loaf, will give him a stone? Or if he asks for a fish, he will not give him a snake, will he? If you then, being evil, know how to give good gifts to your children, how much more will your Father who is in heaven give what is good to those who ask Him!"

Matthew 7:9–11 NASB

Jesus

Our siblings and friends, like Jesus, teach us how to communicate and form healthy companionship with others.

Communication

For there is one God, and there is one mediator between God
and men, the man Christ Jesus, who gave himself as a ransom
for all, which is the testimony given at the proper time.

1 Timothy 2:5–6

For Christ also suffered once for sins, the righteous for the un-
righteous, that he might bring us to God, being put to death in
the flesh but made alive in the spirit.

1 Peter 3:18

Companionship

"No longer do I call you servants, for the servant does not
know what his master is doing; but I have called you friends,
for all that I have heard from my Father I have made known
to you."

John 15:15

"Come to me, all who labor and are heavy laden, and I will
give you rest."

Matthew 11:28

Holy Spirit

Mothers, like the Holy Spirit, are most often our comforters
and instructors.

Comfort

So the church throughout all Judea and Galilee and Samaria
had peace and was being built up. And walking in the fear of
the Lord and in the comfort of the Holy Spirit, it multiplied.

Acts 9:31

Likewise the Spirit helps us in our weakness. For we do not know what to pray for as we ought, but the Spirit himself intercedes for us with groanings too deep for words.

Romans 8:26

Instruction

"And when they bring you before the synagogues and the rulers and the authorities, do not be anxious about how you should defend yourself or what you should say, for the Holy Spirit will teach you in that very hour what you ought to say."

Luke 12:11–12

"But the Helper, the Holy Spirit, whom the Father will send in my name, he will teach you all things and bring to your remembrance all that I have said to you."

John 14:26

"When the Spirit of truth comes, he will guide you into all the truth, for he will not speak on his own authority, but whatever he hears he will speak, and he will declare to you the things that are to come."

John 16:13

As you can see, so much of what Father God provides for us is similar to how fathers provide for their children. In most families, it is the mother who is the comforter and early-years teacher, and it is with our friends and siblings that we learn communication (bartering/posturing) and companionship. If you find any hindrances in your connection with Father God, Jesus or the Holy Spirit, pray and see if there are any lies you believe about Him, others or yourself. To walk free from fear, you must cultivate a strong relationship with the Trinity. We serve one God, but we need to honor the fact that He is made up of three Persons who uniquely provide for our needs.

GROUP DISCUSSION QUESTIONS

1. Is there any fear in your life?
2. If so, can you name or describe that fear?

ACTIVATION PRAYERS

1. Ask Father God if there is any fear in your life.
2. If He says yes, ask what word would describe this fear.
3. Ask Him where you first experienced this fear.
4. Forgive the person or people who brought this fear into your life.
5. Ask Him what lie this person or situation taught you about yourself, others or God.
6. Hand to God the lie you learned.
7. Ask Him what His truth is regarding the lie.

DECLARATIONS

1. I am fearfully and wonderfully made (see Psalm 139:14).
2. I am a temple for the Holy Spirit who resides in me (see 1 Corinthians 6:19).
3. I will not be afraid (see Psalm 118:6).
4. I will not be moved (see Psalm 62:6).

Power

But I will come to you soon, if the Lord wills, and I will find out not the talk of these arrogant people but their power. For the kingdom of God does not consist in talk but in power.

1 Corinthians 4:19–20

3

Why Power Gets Removed
from the Shelf

"The thief comes only to steal and kill and destroy. I
came that they may have life and have it abundantly."

John 10:10

Years ago, I met with a pastor named James whose father had also been in ministry. James had grown up in the church and enjoyed serving, but there was always a nagging fear that told him he would lose it all. An associate pastor before James had fallen into sin, and each Sunday before the service, negative thoughts would appear: *You're no better than the other leader! You're an accident waiting to happen.* When he told his wife about the struggles, they prayed together and agreed he should schedule a Sozo session. A change was needed.

"Honey," he remembered saying, "I can't shake this feeling that I'm about to lose everything."

As I began my session with James, I heard the Holy Spirit say, *He needs to renounce the lie that he will fall into sexual sin like the previous leader.*

I took the Spirit's prompt and asked James, "Do you mind if we ask Jesus some questions?"

"Not at all," he said.

"Go ahead and ask: Jesus, is there a lie I am believing about myself?"

James quickly repeated the prayer. After a few seconds of silence, I asked, "Did you hear, see or sense anything?"

"Yes," he said.

"What was it?"

"Jesus said that I'm afraid of failure. That I'll end up just like the leader before me."

"How does that make you feel?"

"Scared."

"Repeat after me: Jesus, I renounce the lie that I am susceptible to the same attacks that took out my previous leader. I renounce the lie that You won't protect me. Jesus, what truth do You want me to know?"

James prayed for a moment, then looked up.

"What did you hear, sense or see?"

"I don't know. I hear one thing and sense another."

"Okay," I said. "Let's try something else. Ask: Jesus, is there a fear I am believing?"

Without even praying, James said, "Yes. That God won't protect me."

"Ask Jesus where you think you learned this lie."

James prayed for a moment, then said, "My father."

"Repeat after me: I choose to forgive my earthly father for not helping me feel protected. I release him from being absent in my life and for not always being there when I needed him. I renounce all partnerships with fear and command it to leave, in Jesus' name. Jesus, what's Your truth?"

James prayed. After a few seconds, I asked, "Are you hearing, seeing or sensing anything?"

"Yes," he said, sighing. "I see Him covering the church and me from the enemy."

"How does that make you feel?"

"Pretty good," James said, smiling. "And *very* protected."

How Power Gets Removed

There are two common ways power gets removed from our shelves. The first, as in James's story, involves our partnering with a lie. Mostly this occurs at a subconscious level where we might not even realize we have partnered with a lie until it manifests outwardly. The second involves our power being stolen by someone else through control or abuse.

James came into his session feeling far from powerful. By the end, however, he felt loved, chosen and, above all else, protected. James lost his power by partnering with the enemy's schemes of feeling vulnerable. Fortunately, by seizing God's truth, James was able to break free and stand in the reality that he was protected.

We, too, can hand over our power by partnering with the enemy's lies. In James's case, the lie was *I'm not worthy of being protected*. In our own lives, the enemy's schemes will be specific to his attacks against us.

When the disciples cried out to Jesus during the storm, they were believing a lie. Thoughts like *We are all going to drown* were in complete control of their peace. How do we know this? Because when the disciples woke Jesus, they said, "Teacher, do you not care that we are perishing?" God's truth was "I will not leave you or forsake you," but the lie of *You are unsafe* was the belief with which they partnered (Mark 4:38; Joshua 1:5).

We have a choice in all situations to partner with either the enemy's deceptions or the Father's truth. Obviously, the latter is the healthier route. By always keeping your eyes on the Father, you prepare yourself for peace. This posture helps you see your situations from His perspective, which is above—not through—life's stormy situations.

Our power can be stolen in a second way. In situations of victimization, our power gets removed forcibly by others. This is what happens in cases of physical, sexual or emotional abuse. Children are particularly susceptible to this violence and can learn early in life that they are powerless.

If we look throughout history, we can see countless examples of victimization—people trying to steal power. In the case of dictatorships, we see governments using their power to silence the masses. This gives whoever is in charge a false sense of control—and I do mean false. As history has proven, oppressed people eventually begin to complain, speak out and revolt. This phenomenon has occurred in ecosystems of every size—from as small as a married couple to entire nations. I am sure it will continue to manifest itself until Christ's return.

As you can tell, stealing power does not lead to a healthy outcome. When open communication and freedom are not allowed, people use their power in inappropriate ways.

This reminds me of a sermon I gave years ago on the abundance of social agendas coming against the Church. After the message, my son Tim took me aside and said, "Mom, I agree with what you are saying, but you need to be careful. You sound angry."

At first I was frustrated. How could my son not agree with me that this was a big deal? But after thinking about it, I realized he was right. Although I was speaking the truth, an unhealthy spice was seasoning my recipe. I was angry. Because of my inability to stop the ungodly social, religious and sexual attacks thrust upon our churches and families through media, education and politics, feelings of helplessness opened a door to fear. I felt the world was being "swept away" by accepted immorality. Since I had allowed fear to enter into my world-view, I had partnered unintentionally with the spice of anger to make myself feel powerful. This was what my son had experienced in my sermon. If we want to change the world's agendas, we will have to do so from a place of peace—not fear and anger.

Thankfully, God has a plan, and no amount of victimization or stolen power can keep us from stepping into our destinies. If you need encouragement or inspiration to pray for lost power, here are some verses:

> "Thus says the LORD, the God of David your father: I have heard your prayer; I have seen your tears. Behold, I will heal you."
>
> 2 Kings 20:5

> "Whoever causes one of these little ones who believe in me to sin, it would be better for him if a great millstone were hung around his neck and he were thrown into the sea."
>
> Mark 9:42

> "For nothing is hidden that will not be made manifest, nor is anything secret that will not be known and come to light."
>
> Luke 8:17

Powerless Voices

Sometimes people learn to partner with powerlessness as they navigate an early home life. Lies get embedded that create a mindset of powerlessness that follows them into adulthood. This is exactly what happened with Sandy, a middle-aged woman who came to me for a Sozo session. For years Sandy had been struggling with her marriage. Her spouse and teenage son constantly ganged up on her and made her feel bullied. If she tried to defend herself, her husband would just say, "Stop complaining. Can't you see how good you have it?"

Doing some digging with the Holy Spirit, Sandy and I discovered that when Sandy was a little girl, she had not been allowed to have an opinion. When she tried to express her views, her dad would simply shrug and say, "Too bad. That's how we do things around here." Eventually, these interactions taught her a lie—*I don't have a voice.* Sandy carried this mindset into adulthood and ultimately into her marriage.

By the end of our session, Sandy and I had walked through forgiveness regarding her father, husband and son. We came up with a plan to help her communicate bravely to get her needs met.

Losing Control

It is important to realize that voids will always be filled. Unknowingly, Sandy had given up her right to speak, which allowed her husband and son, both strong-willed people, to step into the void she had created. Had Sandy not carried the lie of powerlessness, it would have been much harder for her spouse to intimidate her into silence. Her relationship with her son would also have been different, because she would have raised him to respect her voice rather than to discount it.

A major way that voids are created is through panic. When we partner with panic, we broadcast a need into the atmosphere to grab at whatever is available to help get us through the fearful situation. This broadcast is sent out much like a beacon of a radio station that alerts the unseen realm to offer ways to fill the void.

Although God is always willing and able to step in to cover us, so is the enemy. The most common spice we grab when panicking is control. Interestingly, I find that the most control-ling people I know are also the most fearful. Beneath their bra-vado is an intense panic that screams, *Something bad is about to happen!*

Unfortunately, what sells in the news today is catastrophe and conflict. I have watched when storms are about to hit a country and, even when the weather is calm, the newscasters continue to point out what could happen rather than what is happening presently. They continue to stimulate an atmosphere of panic/fear so people will stay tuned in. It is a focus on fear rather than on God's ability to rescue. The way we stay free from fear in possible catastrophic situations is to seek God and to then step into line with what He is saying about it. In my book *Shifting Atmospheres*,[1] I go into this concept in more detail.

The Bible says that the disciples were so afraid that when they woke Jesus, who was sleeping in the stern of the boat during the storm, they said, "Teacher, do you not care that we are perishing?" (see Mark 4:38). Their inability to control the storm left them vulnerable to fear, whereas Jesus, the Prince of Peace, was able to rebuke the storm and cause it to cease. Jesus was not afraid of the storm because He was never "out of" control. The peace inside Him was bigger than the gales that came against Him. Senior Pastor Bill Johnson of Bethel Church in Redding, California, summarizes this point in a wonderful way, saying, "You will only have authority over the storms you can sleep through."

While we see in Mark 4:38 that the disciples partnered with fear when they experienced a great storm, we can also find multiple examples of God's people partnering with faith and peace in the midst of possible catastrophe.

One example we see is with King Jehoshaphat, who was on the brink of an invasion from his enemies. He was afraid but sought the Lord for wisdom and had his people fast and pray for favor. Eventually, God invaded the situation and brought victory.

As I have gone through life, I have discovered that peace from God is not the absence of conflict, but rather the presence of security in all of life's situations. Just like in the story of Elisha where heaven's armies outnumbered the Syrians, setting our sights on heaven gives us supernatural peace:

> When the servant of the man of God rose early in the morning and went out, behold, an army with horses and chariots was all around the city. And the servant said, "Alas, my master! What shall we do?" He said, "Do not be afraid, for those who are with us are more than those who are with them." Then Elisha prayed and said, "O LORD, please open his eyes that he may see." So the LORD opened the eyes of the young man, and he saw, and behold, the mountain was full of horses and chariots of fire all around Elisha.
>
> 2 Kings 6:15–17

We serve the Lord of Hosts. When you are feeling overwhelmed by the enemy, ask Him to reveal to you His reinforcements. Because you are a child of the King, it is impossible for you ever to be alone in any situation.

Caleb's Story

"Can I ask you something?" Caleb asked.

Caleb, a new client, was trying to manage the amount of stress in his life. A recent graduate from university, he was losing sleep because of the strain of not being able to find a job.

"Sure," I said. "What's bothering you?"

"I went to school thinking I'd have a career by now, but I'm in so much debt! No one's hiring, and my friends who didn't even graduate from high school are making twice what I make. What the heck is going on?"

"Why don't we ask Father God and see what He has to say?"

Caleb sighed, obviously wanting a quicker answer.

I gave him time to relax before asking, "Do you remember the last time you felt powerful? Let's see if we can find a lie you are believing that is making you feel powerless."

Caleb prayed and asked Jesus for His thoughts on the issue. "I just heard that I am believing the lie that I've got to make things happen. But that doesn't make sense. Isn't my success up to me?"

"Why don't we ask Jesus?" I replied. "Repeat after me: Jesus, is my financial success up to me?"

Caleb repeated the prayer and grinned.

"Jesus says it's His job. I can relax."

"How does that make you feel?"

"Less stressed."

"Repeat after me: Jesus, forgive me for putting too much pressure on myself. I hand self-sufficiency to You and command stress to go, in Your holy name."

Caleb repeated the prayer and sat back feeling a heavy weight lift off him.

"Jesus, what truth do You want me to know about my situation?"

Caleb heard God answer, "*You prepare and keep moving forward. I will open the doors for you as you step.*"

Whenever we partner with a lie, we open ourselves up to a battle with fear. Caleb had partnered with self-sufficiency and a mindset of works, even moving into a sense of entitlement because he had worked so hard. This took his eyes off God the provider and put all the expectation for success on his own shoulders. The Bible, however, tells us not to rely on ourselves but rather to "trust in the LORD with all your heart, and do not lean on your own understanding. In all your ways acknowledge him, and he will make straight your paths" (Proverbs 3:5–6).

Conclusion

As you go through your week, remember that the Word of God is true. If you bring your struggles to God in prayer, the "peace of God, which surpasses all understanding, will guard your [heart] and your [mind] in Christ Jesus" (Philippians 4:7).

GROUP DISCUSSION QUESTIONS

1. Can you relate to any area of your life where you have felt or currently feel powerless?
2. Can you remember a time when you felt as if your life was out of control?

ACTIVATION PRAYERS

1. Ask the Holy Spirit to show you any area in your life where you are feeling powerless.
2. Ask Jesus if there are any lies you are believing about this situation.
3. Ask Him if there is someone you need to forgive.
4. Forgive anyone Jesus reveals to you.
5. Ask Him what truth He wants to tell you that will help you combat your fear of being powerless.
6. Ask the Holy Spirit to show you any lies you are believing that are making you feel out of control.
7. Ask Him if there is anyone you need to forgive regarding these lies.
8. Forgive anyone the Holy Spirit brings to mind.
9. Ask Him what truth He wants to show you about your current situation.

DECLARATION

1. I take every thought captive to the obedience of Christ (see 2 Corinthians 10:5).

2. My voice is both pertinent and powerful.

3. Since Jesus is in control of my life (and I am not), I will not partner with fear (see Matthew 6:25–34).

4. I can do all things through Christ who strengthens me (see Philippians 4:13).

4

Powerless Substitutes

When our recipes/formulas are off balance, we pick up ungodly spices to try to create an equilibrium. We might lean toward substitutes that make us feel powerful, like rage, control or manipulation. Or we might try substitutes that help us feel desired, like fantasy or lust. Each of these spices gives us an artificial sense of power, and since they are not from God, they rarely help us equal out our formulas against fear. While these spices do make us feel powerful in the moment, they cost us in the end. Even though substitution seems to solve our pain temporarily, it will always bring us back into a cycle of powerlessness.

Jerry remembered seeing the color red. What he did not remember was how he ended up standing over his wife, fists clenched, observing the ruins of their tattered apartment. Soon the police were at his door, escorting him out to the cruiser and jamming him in.

Scrunched inside the vehicle, Jerry looked back at his apartment wondering, *What happened?*

~~~

Lindsay was angry with Ron. No matter how well she tried to communicate, he could not understand that what he was saying hurt her heart.

"You're such a jerk," she said, slamming the bedroom door behind her.

Lying on her bed, she thought, *Just tell him how you feel. Lay it out. Thick and thin.* Ideas swirled in her mind until— *Aha!—That's it. I'm not going to tell him. I've had it.*

Lindsay hurried to her closet, pulled out a big purple suitcase and started stuffing it with clothes.

I'll show Ron how it feels to be hurt. We'll see how well he can survive without me.

~~~

Dana was tired of cleaning up after the kids, making meals and being stuck with "baby duty."

Is this my life now? she thought, collapsing on the couch. *If my kids were easier to handle, if we had more money or if I had gotten a career going first, this would be so much easier.*

Stressed, Dana went to the store and picked up an armload of romance novels. If George was not going to help her ease the stress, these stories would.

~~~

Bruce was tired of his wife not meeting his sexual needs. He was frustrated with their lack of connection, and nothing he tried seemed to be working.

Well, he thought, sitting down at his computer, *if she is not going to meet my needs, I'll get them met another way.*

These are just a few examples of the ways people turn to substitute spices, such as sex, silence, fantasy and rage, to try to bring power back into their lives. But when we pick up ungodly spices to self-medicate, we never truly find the balance we need to combat fear. In this chapter we will look at many key substitutes and see how a balance of ingredients can bring freedom.

Sexual Sins

According to online statistics, more than forty million Americans visit pornographic sites on a regular basis.[1] These people retreat to the sewers of sexual fantasy as a form of self-medication. It is this retreat that causes problems like "a likelihood of acting aggressively towards members of the opposite sex" and greatly reduces a person's ability to hold healthy opinions on sex and relationships with members of the opposite sex.[2] I do not know about you, but that sounds like false power to me.

Like any addiction, a turn toward pornography tries to nurse a specific need. Working over the past few decades with people who have struggled with this issue, I have found that sexual addictions often come from a person's lack of feeling powerful and the need to take control over his or her life.

Other counselors have found this as well. My oldest son, Cory, was ready to lead his first Sozo session. He had recently passed the Sozo training with flying colors and was eager to see what the Lord would do. He had heard the first person he was going to meet with was a senior leader from a fairly large church.

Oh, thank goodness, he thought. *I'll get an easy one.*

When the door opened, a handsome middle-aged man came in. After politely exchanging pleasantries, Cory sat back and said, "Well, I hope you're ready for a quick Sozo."

"How's that?"

"You're the leader of a huge, successful ministry. I bet there's not much you'll be needing from me."

"Oh, boy," the leader said. "You have no idea. I've struggled with a need for affection my entire life, and it hasn't changed with success. I'm happily married, but whenever I meet an attractive female congregant, I instantly have a strong attraction to her. On top of that, I've been stuck in a cycle of pornography. I can't seem to go more than three days without it. It's gotten so bad that the elders have taken the computer away and asked me to go on probation until this gets figured out."

Note to self, Cory thought. *Being a powerful leader does not always equate to being healthy or having a quick Sozo session.*

~~~~~~~~~~

Pornography and lust can be hard to shake, because like other addictions, they create a false sense of identity/power. This is how it was with a man I counseled years ago. When Paul came in for his Sozo session, he was ready to confess everything. In fact, his first remark was to inform me that he had been stuck in a vicious cycle of sexual addiction.

When I asked him when he had first partnered with pornography, he said it was when he was a young man, right after his father had passed away and he had been forced to become the "man" of the house. My first reaction was to think, *Oh, something happened sexually between him and his mother,* but this was not the case. Paul began telling me about a memory God had been showing him from that time period. His father had just passed away, and Paul was being forced to take care of his father's chores on the farm. In this specific memory, God reminded Paul of how he often had to carry fifty-pound sacks of feed to the animals.

As we asked the Lord to show Paul where God was in this memory, Paul began to cry.

I asked, "What's God showing you?"

Paul said, "I see Jesus putting His shoulder under the sack of feed and lifting off most of the weight. Now we're carrying the bags side by side."

I tried to move on, but he stopped me with much louder sobs and said, "Stop. You don't understand what He is showing me."

I thought, *No, I guess not*, so I let him continue. After what seemed like a long time, he collected himself and sat up straight, signifying he was ready to move on.

After a moment, I asked Paul to repeat after me, "Jesus, what in the heck does that memory have to do with sexual sin?"

Paul repeated this and chuckled through his tears.

"I get it," he said. "It was during this time that I found pornography in the barn. When I was feeling too little for the job, pornography was the only way I could feel like a man."

What an amazing revelation this was for both of us! Pornography, although a sexual sin, had not begun in his life through a sexual need but rather a need to feel powerful.

The problem with opening a door to sexual sin for any reason is that the enemy does not just stop pestering you with one taste. He continues until you are completely hooked:

> With much seductive speech she persuades him; with her smooth talk she compels him. All at once he follows her, as an ox goes to the slaughter, or as a stag is caught fast till an arrow pierces its liver; as a bird rushes into a snare; he does not know that it will cost him his life.
>
> Proverbs 7:21–23

As we shared in the story about Cory and his first Sozo session, being a powerful leader does not always guarantee a healthy lifestyle or a quick Sozo session. Cory continued with the pastor who came for help with pornography. He asked, "What's the Lord telling you now?"

The senior leader's head was hung low, shame growing.

"Repeat after me," Cory said. "Jesus, what lie am I believing?"

"He says"— the leader was almost choking on his words— "that I'm afraid of failing. That I feel powerless and look to my own strength to carry out responsibilities."

"Repeat after me," Cory said. "Jesus, what truth do You want me to know?"

The pastor began to cry harder. "He is saying that I don't need to be afraid. As His son, I can give my fear of failure to Him. He forgives me and is showing me a beautiful red and yellow horizon."

"What does this mean to you?"

As the pastor looked up, astonished, he said, "It's my future! It's going to be a new day!"

Both of these men had retreated to pornography as a way of escaping their fears of inadequacy. Because their sins came not simply from a need for sexual pleasure but from a place of powerlessness, they were unable to break free from addiction until truth was revealed and "true power" was placed back on their shelves. I should mention here that I got a phone call from Paul five years after our session, and he told me, "I have never struggled with sexual sin since." Praise Jesus!

Before the women readers get too riled up about men and their issues with pornography, let us look at a way that some women attempt to quiet their own struggles with powerlessness.

I have found that many women partner with a spirit of fantasy to give them a sense of *I'm okay* when they are feeling abandoned or powerless. Romance novels are seen as an appropriate way for women to help balance out a loss of power. While men tend to gravitate to pornography, I find that women slide more easily into agreement with a spirit of fantasy. Since this issue crosses over into a false spice for love as well, I will leave further discussion on it for another chapter.

What I will address here is how some women have turned to wielding their sexuality as a form of power—as a way to control men and to meet their own needs. Women who do this have often learned it in childhood, where a sexual abuser confused their views on sexuality.

Usually when children grow up with sexual abuse, there is confusion attached to their sexuality. This can open a door to many physical and spiritual attachments. The physical attachments come into play when they get older and engage in sexual sins, and the spiritual door is opened when they believe and agree with demonic lies about sexuality. Being victimized as children, however, does not always leave them victimized as adults.

Sometimes, as adults, they partner with a predator spirit to equal out their recipe from the fear of being victimized. This is not usually done on a conscious level but rather a subconscious one. The body's confusion of heightened sexuality attaches to a demonic force of control where the once abused victim becomes a dominant sexual partner. I believe this is part of the reason for the success of the "sexual liberation" industry where women begin to wield power through S&M practices. But this is not true power. Let me show you what I mean.

Coming in for a Sozo session, Veronica, a new believer, was ready and willing to renounce all sexual sins she had committed previously. As we went through that part of the "Four Doors" tool, she asked God to forgive her for partnering with sexual sin. The "Four Doors" tool in Sozo is used to categorize the four ways in which the demonic realm entices us to partner with sin. The four categories are fear, hatred, sexual sin and the occult. Next, we broke all soul ties to her partners and asked God to wash her clean spiritually, mentally and physically. After this, I asked how she felt. I was surprised when she said, "Sad."

We asked the Lord to show her why she felt this way, and He revealed to her a picture of a trophy case with all her ex-partners lined up as awards. He revealed to her that all of her sexual experimentation was a form of wielding ungodly power over her partners. I asked her where she learned this desire for sexual control, and God took her to early memories of sexual abuse. God then showed her how she had partnered with the same predator spirit that her early abusers had in order to try to combat further victimization.

After God revealed these truths, Veronica forgave her abusers and asked Jesus to forgive her for partnering with a predator spirit. We then broke all agreement to both the human abuser and the evil spirit that had attached to her. Instantly, her countenance brightened.

After that, when I asked Veronica how she felt she said, "Clean."

Superiority

Superiority was a false power spice I picked up at an early age. I found myself using it as a way to protect myself from being threatened by questions from others. I learned this probably from never being able to win an argument against my extremely intelligent brothers. To protect myself from the fear of being wrong, I added to my tool belt the idea of superiority. This was my ability to appear smarter than others, to be better at sports and to be able to get the highest grades in school so I could feel like a powerful person.

Instead, what it did was create a layer of protection that kept others at bay. For much of my childhood I used this spice, and it carried over into my Christian walk as an adult. Within the context of being an adult, superiority took on a different shape—a religious spirit. Even now when I see people carrying the "holier than thou" attitude, I am reminded of my own past with superiority.

This caused tension for me in my early days at Bethel Church. I was seeking God earnestly and felt frustrated that I could never seem to connect with Him. I remember standing in the prayer line every week for two years waiting for God's touch while I watched everyone else fall under the power of the Holy Spirit.

Finally, one day in the prayer line, after having had an internal dialogue with the Lord, I felt convicted about the possibility that I might have betrayed Him if the opportunity had presented itself. I repented and thought, even though I felt courageous and powerful, I might have been like Peter who, although seen by many of us as a powerful disciple, denied Christ when confronted after Jesus had been taken from the Garden.

Out of nowhere, I heard, *You wouldn't have denied Me.*

Wow! I thought. *God's finally talking to me! And even He thinks I'm courageous.*

I heard His voice again. *In My day, kiddo, you wouldn't have been asked the question.*[3]

Why? I thought. *Why not?*

In My day, He went on, *you wouldn't have been a disciple. You would've been a Pharisee.*

Ouch. Talk about a royal spanking. No wonder I was having a hard time connecting with the Holy Spirit. My agreement with superiority kept blocking my ability to hear and follow Him.

Rage

Jerry sat in the back of the police cruiser, rain sloshing on the windshield. A police officer stood at the apartment door speaking with his wife. Jerry looked at his hands, bruised and sprinkled with blood, but *whose*? Jerry stared ahead at the grated window separating him from the front of the car. He knew this was a symbol of his future. This time he had gone too far. Nothing could save him now.

Jerry's story is not random. Studies show that one in every ten Americans has anger problems. These are not just slight bouts of frustration, but actions that are "impulsive, out of control, destructive, or harmful."[4] I find that rage generally enters a person's life in one of three ways: (1) like Helen, blowing up after being forced to stay silent; (2) when either a parent, guardian or one in authority models this to children as a normal response; or (3) as a result of trauma.

Children who grow up with a raging parent learn to view rage as an acceptable form of communication. Easily, the next generation steps in to accept this destructive pattern of anger. This "normal" makes it difficult in later years for them to suppress rage because it is the standard way they have always functioned. It is also difficult to discern as being inappropriate behavior until it manifests in front of others who are willing to confront it. Others may acknowledge how rage harms their families, but they are unable to suppress it. Because they grow up seeing the one with rage as the most powerful person in the family, they throw this spice into the mix to balance their situations when they feel as if their own power is lacking.

One day, a boy was brought to me by a friend in ministry for prayer. The boy had been removed forcibly in restraints from his school by policemen. Sitting with the boy named Toby, this friend in ministry, Sue, asked him what he remembered had happened prior to being tackled by the police. Toby told Sue that he remembered being picked on by some students, being afraid and then letting out his "bear" that he kept in a cage for such occasions.

Obviously, this young boy had picked up a demonic agreement with rage. He had seen the power that both of his parents had wielded with it. Toby went on to tell Sue that he knew it was a demon, but he was okay with it because it protected him when God could not.

Sue asked Toby if he would be willing to ask Father God some questions. Toby said, "Yes."

Sue had Toby ask Father God if there was anyone he needed to forgive. Instantly, Toby heard, *Your family*. In the prayer, Toby forgave his family for the violence happening in his home. Toby told God how they made him feel powerless and unprotected. Sue then asked Jesus to show Toby where He was during these scary times. Toby saw Jesus shielding Him from the violence so that he would not be harmed as well.

Sue led Toby through more similar situations. In each one, Jesus showed Toby how he had not been forsaken or left alone. Toby left the session with homework. He was to continue connecting to Jesus and to find Him whenever he felt afraid.

When Toby came back, Sue asked how the exercises had gone.

"Much better," Toby said.

He told Sue that he had done all his homework, and that Jesus had shown him all the times He had been with him. Sue asked if he felt confident of God's protection and, if so, would he be willing to let the bear go?

Toby answered, "Oh, I let the bear go days ago when Jesus told me I wouldn't need him anymore."

For me, rage was not something I witnessed as a child, but rather a tool I picked up along the way. It was not until I had children of my own that I learned to partner with rage, and sometimes I used it to control my younger, strong-willed son.

My kids labeled my rage *Nanoo Mom* from a cartoon sketch of *Calvin and Hobbes*. This is the cartoon where Calvin, a little boy, has a stuffed animal, Hobbes, whom he blames for all his mischief. In one of the clips, Calvin breaks an item in his home and his mom becomes a robot and starts shouting at him. He yells to Hobbes, "Run. It's the mom from the planet Nanoo." When reading this, my boys looked up and said, "We know that mom."

Over the years, I gained more and more control over my outbursts, but I did not get complete freedom until the Lord revealed to me its origin. One day while I was folding clothes, Cory stomped by in the hallway declaring, "I'm just going to kill myself!" This type of eruption had come often from him in moments of frustration and perceived failure. Just as I had often repented for anger, Cory had repented for partnering with a spirit of suicide. Neither of us, though, had gotten complete freedom.

I stood there feeling helpless and asked God, "What am I going to do? I can't follow my son around the rest of his life breaking off word curses." Instantly, I had a vision of my grandparents growing up in the Great Depression, and I remembered my grandfather talking about going to bed hungry as a child and wondering if he would get to eat the next day.

I heard the Lord say, *Your grandparents partnered with a catastrophic spirit*. He then showed me how their children had also partnered with the same spirit. Then God said, *Cory is partnering with a catastrophic spirit by aligning himself with the spirit of suicide as a way to combat his feelings of hopelessness.*

I was blown away. We had renounced agreement with suicide but never with a catastrophic spirit. I stood there perplexed and told God, "Wow, what a miracle it is that this generational spirit skipped me!"

He simply replied, *It would have been a miracle, indeed, had it skipped you. You don't have an agreement with rage,*

Dawna. You use rage to protect yourself from the catastrophic spirit that stirs up fear when you can't control your situations.

I was floored. For years, I had been caught in a cycle of rage, shame, forgiveness, fear, rage, forgiveness and fear again. In response to the Lord's promptings, I forgave my grandparents and their children for partnering with catastrophe and asked God to forgive me for partnering with it as well. After explaining the situation to Cory, he repented for partnering with suicide. Finally, we asked God to forgive us for using rage and threats of suicide as a way to gain control when we felt overwhelmed.

I am happy to announce that since that time I have not raged, and Cory has gained authority over suicide. Cory is a musician, and on his first album, *Someday When I Am Young,* he added the song "Dissipate," which encourages people to break free from suicide. Over the years, hundreds of people have testified to the song's breakthrough anointing.

Invisibility

My husband, Stephen, tells a story about some of the first spices he discovered—invisibility and rage. His journey to discovering them began years ago in the setting of his grandmother's kitchen on her cattle ranch. One day, as a little boy, Steve was banging empty pots and pans together. His grandmother intervened and said, "Stevie, Stevie. Little boys should be seen and not heard."

Seen and not heard. Grandma's phrase dropped like a seed into the soil of Steve's heart and created a link to a powerful spice—invisibility. From that point on, Steve honored others by keeping silent or by stepping aside when he felt like an annoyance.

As my husband grew, he found more ways to use this substitute. One was hiding from bullies. While in grade school,

Steve was one of the smallest kids on campus, so he was an easy target.

For a short time, invisibility worked. At first the bullies seemed to ignore him. But, like all substitutes, invisibility eventually wore out. Soon the bullies began making it their mission to pick on Steve. Week after week they tracked him down and harassed him.

One day the bullies strode up to Steve and another spice came to the rescue. It was one Stephen had seen his father use on a frequent basis, and it appeared in the form of a big red button called "rage." When the bullies closed in, Steve pushed it.

Minutes later, Steve regained consciousness in the principal's office. A bloodied bully sat next to him in tears. The others were gone. Surprised, Steve looked around the room and wondered, *What happened?*

Although Steve tells this story in a comedic way, the point is that when invisibility failed, he turned to a new spice to give him a false sense of power. Rage equaled out his standing on the playground and allowed him to become a tough enemy. It even won him respect amongst his classmates.

"Steve's a great guy," students said later. "Just don't get him mad."

We can laugh at this idea of invisibility, but many people use it in harmful ways. Surveys on drug use state that more than twenty million Americans battle with substance abuse.[5] As a form of escape/invisibility, drug abuse/addiction costs the U.S. close to $200 billion a year in legal/criminal costs.[6] That is one very expensive crutch people are using to hide from their problems.

Invisibility does not just mean an abuse of drugs; it can also be applied to food, sex or money. This spice can involve literally any addiction as long as it has people trying actively to tune out of their lives rather than engage it in a healthy way.

The National Survey on Drug Use and Health calls drug addiction a disease. As a believer, I understand the premise of it being labeled this way, yet I also see a combination of a person's internal need to disappear as well as a supernatural attachment. Here is an interesting quote from the survey specifically on drug abuse:

> Many people don't understand why or how other people become addicted to drugs. They may mistakenly think that those who used drugs lack moral principles or willpower and that they could stop their drug use simply by choosing to. In reality, drug addiction is a complex disease, and quitting usually takes more than good intentions or a strong will. Drugs change the brain in ways that make quitting hard, even for those who want to. Fortunately, researchers know more than ever about how drugs affect the brain and have found treatments that can help people recover from drug addiction and lead productive lives.[7]

I find the road to freedom from drug abuse and addiction is best found in therapy that includes developing new thought processes—rewiring the brain. My friend and co-leader of the Transformation Center in Redding, Yvonne Martinez, has some great teachings on overcoming trauma. We have found that conversing with God and allowing His truths to overwrite our belief systems creates new pathways in our brains that can walk us out of trauma.[8]

International speaker Sy Rogers talks often about this rewiring of the brain.[9] A former sex addict, he radically encountered God's presence after beginning the process to transform himself into a woman. Days before he was set to undergo the procedure, Sy experienced a radical encounter with God that introduced him to Jesus.

This come-to-Jesus moment did not automatically change Sy's sexual thoughts or desires. Even though he had gotten saved, Sy still felt the sinful urges from his past. In the same way habits get reinforced through years of repetition, so did addiction change the neurological pathways in Sy's brain.

Sy found a way to retrain his brain by bringing all his thoughts to the Father, regardless of whether they were good or bad. This allowed him to confront his sinful thoughts head-on and find liberation in having God renew his mind. Sy's process looked like, "Jesus, I really want this, but I want You more."

Sy tells the story of how his healing process was more of a matter of making constant moral choices than outright healing. By rewiring his brain, Sy was able to conquer his sexual desires and embrace his God-given identity of wholeness. This is a great example of what Paul admonishes us to do in 2 Corinthians:

> For the weapons of our warfare are not of the flesh, but divinely powerful for the destruction of fortresses. We are destroying speculations and every lofty thing raised up against the knowledge of God, and we are taking every thought captive to the obedience of Christ.
>
> 10:4–5 NASB

Silent Treatment

A passive-aggressive substitute for power is when a person uses the "silent treatment" to exhibit false power. People may argue that this silent treatment is really a way for them to take time to process hurt emotions, but I have seen how powerfully controlling withdrawing from relationships can be.

When feeling hurt by others, it makes sense to draw back to a safe distance. It is also important, however, not to retreat into our caves where others have to draw us out. In that case, the offended person appears to be skulking in the corner and withholding affection until the offender makes proper amends.

74

This is a common way people partner with a spirit of control to protect themselves from pain. I would say it is a form of partnering with a victim spirit—used in an unconscious way to control perceived bullies.

My friend Ellen recounts how, as she was praying through fear, God showed her an arcade game. In the game, a gopher popped his head up and she had to to whack it with a baton. Some people know this game as *Whack-a-Mole*. God revealed to Ellen that in her early years she had experienced a pattern of being whacked by the opinions of others and that, like the gopher, she had learned to retreat inside herself.

This transferred to Ellen's interactions with her spouse. When she voiced opinions that differed from his, she felt like he would respond by berating her ideas. Instead of continuing to speak up, Ellen began to retreat inside herself and would only "surface" once her husband sufficiently apologized enough for her to feel safe.

In order to break free from her fears, Ellen needed to walk through forgiving those who belittled her opinions. Next, she had to forgive herself for hiding in order to feel safe. Ellen then broke agreement with invisibility and her pattern of retreating when challenged. After that, Ellen had to learn how to open up and give her opinions without expecting harm. Slowly but surely she began to crawl out of her isolation.

Fantasy

One way many women try to balance out powerlessness is to partner with a spirit of fantasy. This can be as blatant as leading a double life or as subtle as picking up romance novels and living vicariously through their pages.

I found out firsthand how dangerous a spirit of fantasy can be. I have always loved reading. When my boys were young, I would sequester myself away during nap times or late evenings and lose myself in the stories. Little by little, I found myself longing for a more fulfilling life than my simple, dull motherhood routine. I eventually began longing for a rescue of my own. This culminated one day when I found myself lying on the sofa internally battling against the choice to leave the boredom of my life and to follow another man whom I had recently met.

As a Christian, I knew this was the wrong choice, but as a bored and exhausted mom, I felt the need to be rescued. I remember lying there running through the scenarios and outcomes of my possible choice and agonizing over how I was about to destroy both my marriage and my boys' pictures of an ideal family. I wish I could say I easily rebuked the enemy, but I felt so miserable that I just did not care about any collateral damage.

Out of nowhere, I remembered lyrics from an Amy Grant song that reminded me that choosing to follow God is not always easy, but when we do, He promises it will work out for our good.

I groaned and simply cried out, "I hope so, Lord."

Much like Sy Rogers, I remember praying, "Lord, if You don't take this choice away, I'm going to choose sin. Please make me a robot that *has* to obey. Please take away my self-will."

Although God did not take away my free will, He did miraculously shut the door to my notion of escape by having the man never contact me again.

Years later, I ran into him accidentally and he remarked how happy I looked. In explanation of why he had not contacted me again, he said, "I just felt like I couldn't break up a marriage. I figured that if you wanted me, you would come find me after your divorce."

Wow! God desired so strongly to rescue me from partnering with the spirit of fantasy that He convicted a nonbeliever not to touch one of His precious families. That is the God we serve.

GROUP DISCUSSION QUESTIONS

1. Is there a pattern in your life from which you have trouble breaking free?
2. Do you resonate with any of the stories in this chapter? If so, which ones?
3. While reading this chapter, have you identified any ungodly spices that you have used to gain lost power? Give an example of what this has looked like.

ACTIVATION PRAYERS

1. Ask the Holy Spirit if there are any ungodly spices you have been using to try to balance out your recipe.
2. If the answer is yes, ask Him where you first learned to value the spice.
3. Ask Him if there is anyone you need to forgive for teaching you this spice.
4. Forgive anyone God reveals to you. (It may even be yourself.)
5. Release that person from any harm done and ask God to release others from harm you have caused by wielding false power.
6. Hand Father God the spice you have been using and ask Him what He wants to give you in exchange.
7. Thank Him for this exchange, then ask Holy Spirit to show you how to wield this new gift in future situations.

8. If you are struggling with sinful desires, admit them to God and ask Him to provide a way of escape for you.

9. Hand Him these desires and ask Him to give you His instead.

DECLARATION

1. The weapons of my warfare are powerful for the tearing down of strongholds (see 2 Corinthians 10:4).

2. I can be honest with God. I can tell Him what I am desiring and can exchange these desires for what He knows is better for me. I *get* to choose righteousness.

3. Bullies are *not* powerful; they are fear-filled, and I am not intimidated by their tactics.

4. Jehovah is my light and salvation. Whom shall I fear? (see Psalm 27:1).

5

Powerfully Alive

For in him the whole fullness of deity dwells bodily,
and you have been filled in him, who is the head of
all rule and authority.

Colossians 2:9–10

God places the ingredient of power on our shelves, but it is our responsibility to keep it there. Issues like fear, lies and demonic mindsets tempt us to remove power, but we must be strong enough to resist attacks. Only then can we keep ungodly spices out of our recipes.

God imparts His power to us as we accept Jesus Christ as our Lord and Savior. Powerlessness, helplessness, poverty mindsets and orphan spirits are just some spices the devil uses to invade our lives if we are not connected to Christ. Even when we do not feel powerful in situations, we can be confident that the weak are strong in the strength of the Lord (see 2 Corinthians 12:10). We are also told that when we "hav[e] done all, to stand firm" and that we can "walk through the valley of the shadow of death" and "fear no evil, for you are with me" (Ephesians 6:13; Psalm 23:4).

Being powerful is a part of our redeemed identities. When we say yes to Jesus, power becomes an aspect of our being. We receive His supernatural blood that "pardons all [our] iniquities . . . heals all [our] diseases . . . and redeems [our lives] from the pit" (Psalm 103:3–4 NASB). Jesus tells us that "all authority in heaven and on earth has been given to me" and that "nothing shall hurt you" (Matthew 28:18; Luke 10:19). When we receive Jesus, we become unstoppable warriors for Him.

As believers, we can be confident in the assignment God has for us, and know that He will guard us and cover us as we walk out our assignments. One of my favorite verses that encourages me to remember the protection of God is Psalm 91. In its opening passages, we are told: "He who dwells in the shelter of the Most High will abide in the shadow of the Almighty. I will say to the LORD, 'My refuge and my fortress, my God, in whom I trust'" (verses 1–2).

Trusting in God allows us not to fear. In this place of not fearing, we can use our voices powerfully to speak out as He directs. In the confidence of being covered by God, we can easily silence the enemy's accusatory lies coming at us without having to be abrupt or abusive to those around us.

Powerful Dreamers

My husband, Stephen, has a powerful message on dreaming. In the message, he encourages the Church to take Sabbath (rest) seriously, for in our moments of rest is when we dream most easily. Dreaming (not the sleeping kind) is what kicks open our imagination and allows us to be partners with God to see what impossibilities He wants us to tackle.[1] Each of us is called to at least one realm of society, whether it is *family, education, religion, government, business, science and technology* or *arts and entertainment*.[2] By turning on our *inner dreamers*, we get to see where God wants us to go, find out what He wants us to do and direct our steps on how to get there.

Some Christians think places like Hollywood, the public education system and the government are lost causes. But what if God is waiting for powerful believers to step up and inhabit these areas? When we study Scripture, we see heroes like Joseph, who served nonbelievers and led them toward movements that helped save God's people (see Genesis 50:20).

If we feel God's commission to go to these places, then we need to embrace our powerful identities and realize we are protected by God. God does not call us out to deep waters and then leave us to drown. He challenges us with opportunities (which we can handle) and guides us along the way. If you feel yourself currently out in the deep surrounded by sharks, remember Psalm 91. Stop and remind yourself about how He promises to shelter you and tuck you under His wings.

We can be out on the front lines of battle and under God's protection at the same time. Remember that David said, "You prepare a table before me in the presence of my enemies" (Psalm 23:5). If you find yourself out in deep water and feel unsafe, ask God to show you what He sees. I guarantee you He will provide an answer that you have missed previously.

Humbly Powerful

Since we can "fear not" due to God's protection, we can speak with confidence. We can silence the enemy's accusations, partner with God and embrace humility. Humiliation is never God's intention for our lives but being powerfully humble is. Humbly walking in God's design is what it means to be powerful.

Proverbs 22:4 tells us, "The reward for humility and fear of the LORD is riches and honor and life."

It is interesting how advancement/promotion in the Kingdom comes through humility. This does not mean thinking less of ourselves or cutting ourselves off from opportunity. It means hearing what God has to say about us, believing Him and walking it out faithfully.

One time my younger son, Tim, was on a university outreach trip. He and some other students were crammed in a bus headed to another city. On this drive, Tim was sitting next to a young, irate woman who was having trouble accepting the idea of an all-powerful, loving God.

"I just think the idea that God is the only way seems arrogant," she said.

"How so?" Tim asked.

"The way God sees Himself as the only way to salvation. It's prideful."

"Well," Tim said, "it's like this. Say you have a cat and a turtle, and the cat really wants to be a turtle. So the cat comes up to the turtle and says, 'Hey, I want to be a turtle just like you.' But the turtle says, 'Sorry, you're a cat.' Is the turtle arrogant or just being realistic?"

I wish I had been there to see the look on this woman's face. I am sure she was miffed, perhaps stunned and maybe even impressed by Tim's rebuttal. God calling Himself the way, the truth and the life is not arrogant; it is just true. You stepping into whom God has called you to be is not arrogant. It should simply be you walking in the truth of who you are.

Danny Silk has a wonderful book on wielding power called *The Culture of Honor*.[3] In it he exposes how we tend to treat people disrespectfully when we do not feel they have adhered to our standards. Instead of responding to people from a place of honor, we often berate, belittle and bully others we deem unworthy of our respect.

Danny points out that honor is not just meant to be given when we feel people have earned it, but rather as an extension of the nature we carry in ourselves. Putting this into practice will keep you from partnering with arrogance—which is thinking of yourself more highly than others. It is okay to think positively of yourself. It is another to discount someone else who seems or appears to be worthless.

Danny's culture of honor teaches that true power looks like allowing others to speak even when they have differing opinions. It is like the principle of free speech laid out in America. Freedom of speech does not mean I get to shut down your voice because I disagree with you. Neither does it mean that my voice is diminished because of something you said with which I disagree. It is meant to create a safe environment for all parties and to give all voices an equal say. Run well, this principle can help to keep everyone in a state of feeling heard. When it is done supernaturally well, it helps everyone on each side feel honored.

I believe it was this very characteristic of God's nature that allowed Christ to confidently and humbly wield His power without sacrificing the truth of His message.

Christ's Secret

When we are confident in who we are in God, we should be more easily able to walk in His likeness. Christ's confidence seemed to flow from knowing His identity as God's beloved Son. Even as a child, Jesus knew who He was and made sure to be about His Father's business:

> After three days they found him in the temple, sitting among the teachers, listening to them and asking them questions. And all who heard him were amazed at his understanding and his answers. And when his parents saw him, they were astonished. And his mother said to him, "Son, why have you treated us so?

Behold, your father and I have been searching for you in great distress." And he said to them, "Why were you looking for me? Did you not know that I must be in my Father's house?" And they did not understand the saying that he spoke to them. And he went down with them and came to Nazareth and was submissive to them. And his mother treasured up all these things in her heart. And Jesus increased in wisdom and in stature and in favor with God and man.

Luke 2:46–52

Jesus' secret was that He knew His assignment and stuck to it. After His death, the disciples carried His dreams forward and passed the baton to us. Perseverance was one of Jesus' strengths, and it plays a powerful role in our understanding of how we become Christians—"little Christs."

Scripture warns us not to give in to the enemy's schemes, but rather to stand in the midst of the battle (see Ephesians 6:13). I have found that perseverance can be tiresome if we do not fully understand what we are persevering for.

Count it all joy, my brothers, when you meet trials of various kinds, for you know that the testing of your faith produces steadfastness. And let steadfastness have its full effect, that you may be perfect and complete, lacking in nothing.

James 1:2–4

Not only that, but we rejoice in our sufferings, knowing that suffering produces endurance, and endurance produces character, and character produces hope.

Romans 5:3–4

Perfection, completeness, character and hope are just some of the promised rewards that are listed in Scripture. Knowing this, the next time you feel resistance, thank the Lord that it is another layer of strength and character He is adding to you.

Perhaps the most powerful of all these rewards is hope. Hope gives us the ability to see our situations not from under affliction but from the heavenly realm where we are seated with Christ (see Ephesians 2:6). It shifts our perspective off of what seems to be hindering us and onto our ability to hear God's strategies. Hope releases us to dream and casts vision for our standings in the midst of every struggle so that we can continue on.

Perseverance also creates confidence. Wielded correctly, confidence can bring us through any situation. Even when we cannot see the end, we can have confidence in Christ, which allows us to put our heads down and move forward. Paul states it this way: "And now, behold, I am going to Jerusalem, constrained by the Spirit, not knowing what will happen to me there" (Acts 20:22). As we remain confident in the power of Christ and our assignment in life, we will not be swayed. We will instead fasten ourselves to the call on our lives and march powerfully ahead.

Conclusion

God has given us powerful tools to use to combat enemy tactics like stress, panic, hopelessness, abuse and fear. Confidence in who we are in Christ, hope and knowing our identity as sons/daughters of God give us the strength needed to persevere and keep moving ahead.

If your ingredient of power starts to run low, ask God what it is you are fearing. Do not pick up false, powerless spices. Instead, listen to the Holy Spirit so you can determine how to dispel enemy lies.

If you feel afraid or find yourself reacting with an old, powerless spice, stop and ask God what lie you are believing. The enemy will try to bait you again and again to partner with fear. I still do this myself, and I am amazed continually at how every time I want to puff up bigger, it is because I am feeling afraid.

This has become my *tell*—my way of knowing that fear is trying to bait me. When I feel this, I ask God to show me any lies I am believing, and then I ask the Lord for His higher perspective. When we stop and ask for wisdom, we find ourselves seated with Christ in the heavenlies and our circumstances take on a much different perspective.

GROUP DISCUSSION QUESTIONS

1. Are you confident in who you are in Christ?
2. Are you confident that Father God is for you and will protect you in all situations?
3. Can you remember a situation where you had to persevere? If so, share where you are now and celebrate how perseverance worked for you.
4. What does it look like to wield power humbly?
5. Can you identify what your *tell* is? If so, what is it?

ACTIVATION PRAYERS

1. Ask the Holy Spirit if there are any lies you are believing about yourself.
2. Ask Him where you learned these lies.
3. Ask Him if there is anyone you need to forgive regarding these lies.
4. Ask Him for His truth.
5. Ask if there are any lies you are believing about Him. If so, then ask the Holy Spirit where you learned this lie.
6. Ask Him if there is someone you need to forgive for teaching you this lie.

7. Ask Him to reveal to you His true nature.

8. Ask Father God to give you insight on how He wants you to live a powerful life.

9. Ask the Holy Spirit to give you one practical way to begin walking out your powerful life.

DECLARATION

1. If I start to respond in an old way, it does *not* mean I have not broken free.

2. New patterns are being created in my life as I forsake old spices and wield true power.

3. I can do *all* things through Christ who strengthens me (see Philippians 4:13).

4. As I follow the Holy Spirit, He keeps me aligned under the shadow of the Almighty (see Psalm 91:1).

5. The weapons of my warfare are not of the flesh but are powerful for the tearing down of strongholds (see 2 Corinthians 10:4).

6. No stronghold I have ever partnered with is stronger than God's grace!

PART 3

Love

Beloved, let us love one another, for love is from God, and whoever loves has been born of God and knows God. Anyone who does not love does not know God, because God is love.

1 John 4:7–8

6

What's Love Got to Do with It?

It is very possible that you have collected some unsavory spices that affect how you give and receive love. These unhealthy spices, in the form of false beliefs about love, can sneak into your thinking without your even being aware that they are present. Recognizing these false beliefs is key to beginning the process of removing them from your life. This chapter describes several examples of troublesome false beliefs. As you read through them, see if you can identify any with which you might have partnered.

Boundaryless Love

Mary came to my office for a Sozo session. She had been diagnosed with early-stage multiple sclerosis and was experiencing both muscle motion issues and extreme levels of pain in her body. She had been prayed for so many times without sensing any relief that she was left with little hope.

As I began to minister, I sensed that she had no real understanding of how boundaries work. Like most Christians, Mary was told, "Just turn the other cheek." I began to ask her questions about her early home life, and what we discovered confirmed my sense of the powerlessness that she felt.

When I asked God to take her to a memory of when she realized that she was not allowed to say no, God showed her several pictures. In these memories, the men of the house got to sit around and watch television while she and her mother hustled around feverishly preparing meals and completing household chores. The Lord then showed her other memories where she had been required to carry heavy loads while her brothers and father looked on directing her assignments. God confirmed that these events in her life trained her to believe she did not have the right to say no.

As we unfurled this deep-seated belief system, we found contrasting memories where she seemed to have been given a pass not to be the family workhorse. In each event, it was because she was physically ill or sick in bed. This left Mary with a belief that I find among many Christians. It is the idea that we are not allowed to say no unless we are physically incapable of performing the requested service.

The Holy Spirit pointed out to Mary that she had made an agreement with frailty in exchange for being able to rest. As Mary forgave her family for teaching her that no was not a word she was allowed to use, we asked the Lord to forgive her for partnering with a spirit of frailty.

After praying this through, Mary looked up and said to me, "I'm going to learn how to say no!"

It is interesting and sad how lies that Mary had believed had hindered many of the healing prayers that she had received over the years. Mary believed that denying her own needs for others kept her in a state of Christian love; however, it actually kept her in a state of oppression. Bill Johnson in his sermon "Sex and the Body" says that "unsanctified mercy empowers sin."[1]

We are called to extend grace, but never to ignore or applaud wickedness. When we partner with a lie that love is silent or nonconfrontational, or when we ignore all beneficial boundaries, we hand over our power to another person. As a result, we forfeit our voices and give him or her control.

Victim Spirit

Years ago, an individual whose spiritual discernment I greatly respect came to visit Bethel Church in Redding, California, and I invited him to join my family for a meal. Over dinner, I asked how he found our spiritual atmosphere. I was expecting him to say, "It's great!" Since we had encountered a spirit of control from many people in our region, my team and I had been working hard to remove it.

To my surprise, he said, "Actually, Dawna, the spirit of control is much stronger than before."

No way! I thought. *We've been breaking off all the controlling spirits we can find. How's this possible?*

When I mentioned my doubts, he explained, "What you're not seeing is the controlling power of a victim spirit."

"Okay," I said, still not understanding fully.

To help me understand, he told me a story. "It's like when you hear a scratching noise on your front door. You go to investigate and find a muddy, mangy dog on your porch. Before you can turn it away, it skulks into your living room and jumps on your couch. Now you are stuck with a dilemma. You need to get the dog off the couch, but every time you try to move it, it whines and whimpers. You feel bad because you don't want to hurt the dog, but you really need it off the furniture.

"The victim spirit," he finished, "is one of the most controlling spirits because when you confront it, you are seeming to hurt the person you are needing to help."

93

Wow! I thought. *This is such great insight.*

Over the years, I have seen this to be true. A victim spirit does not want you to confront it and will do everything possible to pressure you to be "loving."

How many of us have felt powerless to help those carrying a victim spirit? What often happens is that they recoil or lash out at us when we confront them, saying, "You aren't being loving like Christ!"

Fantasy Spirit Revisited

Years ago, I had a friend with whom I would get coffee on a regular basis. She confided in me that her husband was not happy with the time she spent away from the house. She shared that he was even starting to feel a bit jealous of our time together. Over the course of a few months, I watched as she became more and more depressed. It was hard to see my friend so defeated.

One day I remarked that there was a noticeable positive change in her demeanor. She smiled and said, "Yes. I started tutoring a couple of new kids for extra money and they are great." Throughout the next school year, I watched as my friend came back to life.

After time, though, some of our conversation went back to her husband being jealous and passive-aggressive. Her husband's faults had become more obvious to her because she was able to compare how the father of the two boys that she tutored was so different from her husband. We would then spend the rest of the walk talking about this other family—how cute the kids were and what a great dad they had.

Somewhere along the way I started to feel uncomfortable. I confronted her gently on her attachment to this other family. She dismissed my concerns and said it was just great to see how a healthy family lived. As time passed, though, she began to talk about the possibility of leaving her husband to be with this man and his children. Rationally she knew it was wrong, but at the same time it felt right. She did not realize that over time she had come under the influence of a spirit of fantasy that she had allowed into her life.

Thankfully, before she got to the point of leaving her husband, they received counseling and were able to break free from the spirit's hold. I have not forgotten the pull that this spirit had on both of our hearts.

The fantasy spirit holds a carrot out and says, *See what you could have if . . .* and *It really isn't God's desire for you to have to remain in an unhappy marriage.* The fantasy spirit whispers, *You deserve. You can have. This is your only way to happiness.* It is similar to the spirit of Mammon, which is a demonic mindset of greed.[2]

Because fantasy is such a soothing spirit, it can actually deceive those around you into believing the delusion that they will soon be happy even if they follow a sinful course. In the end, the spirit has to be exposed for what it is, and the person under its influence needs to listen to wise counsel. I have a friend named Susan Anderson who has coined a phrase that I have used many times to help people break free from this spirit.

She states simply and gently, "You can't tell me the only way God has set it up for you to get your needs met is to sin. It is against His nature. There has to be another way."

Self-Pity

Jim sat in one of the chairs in my office. His wife had begged him to see me. She had had enough of his self-pity and constant need for over-the-top care. To top it all off, Jim had been physically ill most of their marriage, and she was—as he told it—done with his inability to care for himself. Treading lightly, I asked the Holy Spirit to take him to the first memory he had of being nurtured by his mother.

He scoffed a bit at first and said, "My mother was not a very nurturing person."

I encouraged him to forgive his mom for not providing the care he needed as a child, and he presented his need of being cared for to Jesus. The Holy Spirit then showed him a time when he was very young. In this memory, Jim had just been sent to the hospital with pneumonia. As he recalled this time period, he started to cry.

"I remember this time," he said. "My parents were afraid I would die, so my mom stayed by my hospital bed all night until I got well. Looking back," he continued, "this is the only time I ever felt loved by my mom."

As he said this, a realization struck him. "I get it! I learned to partner with sickness in order to get my needs met. No wonder my wife is sick of me!"

Excitedly, I led Jim through a quick prayer. We asked Jesus to forgive him for partnering with self-pity, and he forgave his wife for not giving in to his manipulation tactics. (This might seem strange, but forgiving someone for what they did, even if they were in the right, brings healing.) He was finally able to understand the consequences of his behavior and he left our session ecstatic. He and his wife could now begin cultivating the healthy communication they had so long desired. A mutually healthy marriage was now in their grasp.

Sexual Perversion

When Veronica came in for a Sozo session, she explained that she had become a Christian a few years earlier but continued to struggle with setting physical boundaries with the men she dated. When we got to the part of the Sozo session that deals with sexual sin, she said simply, "I don't have any."

I was wondering how to proceed when I saw a picture in my mind of a sack of potatoes being passed around from person to person. Since we were at a standstill in the session, I shared this picture, thinking to myself, *Well, maybe she has already asked God to forgive her for all sexual sin, and this picture will move us onto the next path we need to take.*

But her answer took me aback.

"Oh," she said. "Well, do you mean like when I was a child and my dad had sex with me? Then when he was done, how he passed me off to my grandfather? Then after that, one of my uncles? Is that what you meant?"

Nooo, I thought. *That can't be what I meant!*

Throughout her life, Veronica had been so sexually abused by the men in her family that she equated sex with a hug or a handshake. To her, normal affection was not a smile or a hug but the act of sex itself.

I walked her through a prayer of forgiveness that released her family for teaching her that sex was the only way a man could care for her, then asked God to show her His plan for sexuality. She opened her eyes at the end of the prayer and shared excitedly how God had released her from a generational tie to sexual sin. When I saw her years later, she was still walking in the freedom she had received through that revelation.

Like Veronica, many people learn a false sense of love because of abuse in the home. Veronica's paradigm was seeing love and care as sexual; Jim's view equated love with an ongoing need to have nursing care. Within the ministry of deliverance, we often find ourselves praying for people to hand God their prior belief systems regarding love. In place of those old systems, we ask the Lord to reveal His truth.

So many of us have a twisted sense of what love means. Even when we look to the Scriptures for answers, we can apply them inappropriately. This can lead us to believe we are being loving when really we are being deluded. One Scripture I have seen misapplied is in Matthew:

> Hearing that Jesus had silenced the Sadducees, the Pharisees got together. One of them, an expert in the law, tested him with this question: "Teacher, which is the greatest commandment in the Law?" Jesus replied: "'Love the Lord your God with all your heart and with all your soul and with all your mind.' This is the first and greatest commandment. And the second is like it: 'Love your neighbor as yourself.' All the Law and the Prophets hang on these two commandments."
>
> Matthew 22:34–40 NIV

Have you heard, "You can't love others until you learn to love yourself"? Although I believe that this statement is accurate, when it is misapplied, we are misled into a twisted version of self-love that becomes "I deserve." What this leads to is selfishness and entitlement. I think what God is pointing out to us in these verses is that it is natural to want to care for yourself, to self-protect, to work hard and press in to get your needs met. I do not, however, think Jesus is telling us that we need to fall in love with ourselves before we can love others.

I think Jesus is saying, "Just as you are naturally built to pursue your own needs, so you must naturally apply this same drive to others." In fact, many times Jesus came against the "I deserve" and "I'm going to get it for myself" messages. We see this in several of His teachings:

> "Do not lay up for yourselves treasures on earth, where moth and rust destroy and where thieves break in and steal, but lay up for yourselves treasures in heaven, where neither moth nor rust destroys and where thieves do not break in and steal. For where your treasure is, there your heart will be also."
>
> Matthew 6:19–21

Although I believe it is important that we see ourselves as God sees us (redeemed, sanctified and purified by Christ), focusing on ourselves does not lead to greater righteousness. It is in focusing our attention on the Lord that we begin to conform to His image. The form of self-love I adhere to is the reflection of myself I see in God's eyes.

Pornography

Pornography is a bait of the enemy that says, "You can get your love needs met on your own terms." It is a false intimacy that allows you not to need a real relationship. In our relationally disconnected society, pornography is flourishing because it provides a way for people not to have to risk relational failure. Instead, they can connect virtually with anyone without the fear of being rejected.

Ed, a mand who struggled with this, came in for a Sozo session. When I asked what was wrong, he said he struggled daily with pornography and masturbation. As we walked through the Sozo process, I saw shame draped all over him, and he began to cry. I asked him what was wrong, and he said, "God is showing me a time when I was a little boy and my cousin molested me."

Ed forgave his cousin for taking advantage of him, and then his parents for not being there to protect him. Lastly, we broke off soul ties, which are deeply held relational attachments, to his cousin.

Afterward, I had Ed speak to his body and say, "I'm sorry, body, that you were touched inappropriately at a young age and that I didn't know how to stop it. I release you, body, from the confusion of being awakened sexually too soon. I break free of the lie that masturbation and pornography are proper forms of intimacy."

I asked God to remove from Ed's mind every image of pornography and sexual sin and to remove all sexual physical torment that these images had released into his body. We prayed for God to reboot his brain from old patterns and to replace them with how God created him to be. It has been several years since our last meeting and, according to Ed, he is doing extremely well.

———————

I would be remiss not to mention here that when dealing with addictions, we do not just have the client muster up his own will to stop. Rather, we find out why the pattern exists in the first place. Fighting an addiction with your own strength is like picking the rotten fruit off a bad tree. Picking the bad fruit may get rid of the odor, but it will not kill the tree itself. You must uproot the tree to kill the bad fruit. To truly break an addiction, you must uproot both the belief systems that are planted in your heart and the resulting sinful habits that first seeded the addiction.

Jesus tells us that we cannot get bad fruit from a good tree or get good fruit from a bad one (see Matthew 7:18). Bad fruit, as shocking as it is for others to find, is only evidence of a bad tree (mindset/belief system) taking root. Uncovering the root system of rotten trees and then ripping them out is the only way lasting freedom occurs.

Tolerance

There is a spice going around the world today that is a distorted lie from the enemy. Masquerading as love, this spice, called "tolerance," has become a massive wall built up to keep truth out of popular conversation.

Many Christians today are told that their biblical views are intolerant and unloving. This, however, is itself intolerance. Tolerance does not mean that individual values are rejected.

The dictionary says that tolerance is "the ability to tolerate something, in particular the existence of opinions or behavior that one does not necessarily agree with."

That word, by definition, means that both worldly and Christian views get to coexist. Somehow the idea has been warped into a controlling spice. My *having* to be okay with someone training my children in an alternate sexual lifestyle is not loving; it is controlling. My *having* to stay silent to protect the feelings of others while ignoring mine is not equality; it is enslavement. For tolerance to work correctly, it needs to support all voices—not just the ones with which certain people agree.

Unfortunately, many well-meaning people have jumped on the tolerance train, using it to attack those whose morals seem to limit other people's freedoms. What most likely began as a desire to give a voice to a specific belief system has become a chokehold on the Church. Now the enemy's goal is to systematically tighten his grip so he can silence God. Many Christians have been taken by surprise by this assault because they wanted to avoid conflict and appear loving. Because of this choice, they have stopped speaking God's truth into the world.

> Do not love the world or the things in the world. If anyone loves the world, the love of the Father is not in him. For all that is in the world—the desires of the flesh and the desires of the eyes and pride of life—is not from the Father but is from the world. And the world is passing away along with its desires, but whoever does the will of God abides forever.
>
> 1 John 2:15–17

While I believe all voices have a right to be heard, tolerance has been perverted into a weapon to silence religious freedom. I want everyone's voices to hold value, but it is important we stick to God's truth and protect the freedoms we currently (and hopefully will for a long time) enjoy.

Unsavory spices can season our lives with false beliefs. It takes intentional effort to have God help us remove them, but I have seen time and time again that freedom from their influence is possible. This week ask God to help you be aware of your thoughts and to recognize when your recipe is being changed by any of the spices mentioned in this chapter.

GROUP DISCUSSION QUESTIONS

1. Do you resonate with any of the examples in this chapter? If so, which ones?
2. If not, did you get insight into a false belief you may have partnered with regarding love?
3. Give an example of what this spice has looked like in your life.

ACTIVATION PRAYERS

1. Ask the Holy Spirit to show you if you have partnered with an unhealthy spice.
2. Ask the Holy Spirit where you first learned to use this spice.
3. Ask Him if there is anyone you need to forgive for introducing you to this spice.
4. Forgive anyone God reveals to you (it may be yourself).
5. Release that person and yourself from any harm done or for any way you have manipulated others to feel loved.
6. Hand Father God the spice you have been using and ask Him what truth He wants to reveal to you.
7. Thank Him for this exchange and ask the Holy Spirit to show you how to wield this truth.

DECLARATION

1. I do not need to go outside of God's will to get my needs met.

2. I now have the mind of Christ and I understand what love truly is (see 1 Corinthians 2:16).

3. I am adored by Father God, and the Holy Spirit is training me to walk in a new level of love (see Romans 8:15; John 14:26).

7

Keeping Love on the Shelf

Love bears all things, believes all things, hopes all
things, endures all things. Love never ends.

1 Corinthians 13:7–8

Most people recognize that love is sacrificial. Love en-
gages our ability to give kind, helpful instruction.
It requires us to put our full trust in God, and it
requires a mastery of grace. I learned a lot about love while
raising my two boys. Yet child rearing also required the imple-
mentation of both structure and brave communication.

As parents, Stephen and I experienced vast pendulum swings,
from imposing strict boundaries on our children to allowing
their successful failure. Although love weathers all things and
never fails, it was still hard for us to master, because the parental
game changed almost daily.

Some people believe love means staying silent or extending grace without consequences. I, however, see it as a way
to stand firm in our convictions as we call people up to their

best selves. In my years with Sozo, I have seen that both fear of confrontation and lack of proper boundaries can hinder relational growth.

Many Christian women confess that they try to make people they love more like Jesus by praying silently for them. Praying to God is important, but so is communicating your needs. Expecting people to change without ever communicating to them is a set-up for disaster. In fact, secretly working to change a person or a situation is a form of manipulation. Brave communication is important. Reinforced with prayer, it serves as a powerful weapon.

Christ's Confrontation

Christ is the ultimate example of love, but we sometimes fail to recognize how often He engaged in confrontation. If we look closely, we can see how important brave communication was to Christ's ministry:

> "Woe to you, scribes and Pharisees, hypocrites! For you build the tombs of the prophets and decorate the monuments of the righteous. . . . You serpents, you brood of vipers, how are you to escape being sentenced to hell?"
>
> Matthew 23:29–33

> But she came and knelt before him, saying, "Lord, help me." And he answered, "It is not right to take the children's bread and throw it to the dogs."
>
> Matthew 15:25–26

> But he turned and said to Peter, "Get behind me, Satan! You are a hindrance to me. For you are not setting your mind on the things of God, but on the things of man."
>
> Matthew 16:23

Jesus said to him, "Have I been with you so long, and you still do not know me, Philip? Whoever has seen me has seen the Father. How can you say, 'Show us the Father'?"

John 14:9

We were made for relationship with the Lord and with others. It is important that we learn to communicate well with our loved ones, co-workers and friends. Confrontation can be messy, especially if we failed to learn how to do it well in childhood. Developing this skill is necessary to empower love and to keep a fear-free formula on the shelf.

Love Has a Voice

People who did not learn how to communicate properly as children tend to swing between two extremes: the fear of speaking out or the practice of bullying others into silence. I find that most Christians tend to fear speaking out, but I have also seen a handful of leaders who have moved into the practice of bullying. This latter option usually happens when people feel their voices are being silenced. To combat being silenced, they lash out. It is important to avoid both of these extremes so we can develop proper communication skills and protect our fear-free recipes.

As a child, I loved watching the television show *Perry Mason*. In it, a trial attorney, Mason, worked hard to defend his clients—no matter the case. The confrontations were fun for me. Each week Mason's team investigated their client's case and won by outsmarting the opposition's liars. As a child, I was caught up in the spectacle of it all and dreamed that I, too, would someday become a trial attorney. When I got to high school, though, I found out I really did not like debating.

While participating on the high school debate team, I actually enjoyed hearing my opponent's ideas. The problem was that I never had time to check out whether or not my opponent was telling the truth. For all I knew, every argument he or she made was factual. After a few rounds of these debates, I realized that it was rarely the best researcher who won, but rather the person who refused to back down from his or her beliefs. In a way, I learned that bullying made people winners. Today when I watch political debates, the candidates often reinforce this opinion.

As mentioned in the previous chapter, in response to not allowing bullying in social and political settings, tolerance has become an effective battering ram to silence opposing viewpoints. It, however, carries with it its own bullying tactic. To avoid social and political abuse, those being accused of racism, xenophobia or bigotry (I cannot keep up with all the labels) shrink back into silence.

I believe the Church has fallen prey to this tactic and has gradually retreated from society to the point that it has lost most of its verbal impact. Religion is not perfect, and people using the name of Jesus have not always represented Him well, but employing the opposite extreme of cowering in silence is far from the answer.

Absolutes

The devil wants us to partner with the lie that there are no absolutes and that "anything goes," but the Word of God states otherwise. As much as the world does not want us to think they exist, there is a heaven and a hell. There are absolutes. The Church's decision to remain silent in the face of ungodliness has not been loving. Instead, I see it as cowardice. Believers are to speak with grace and boldness, gentleness and truth:

> "You are the salt of the earth, but if salt has lost its taste, how shall its saltiness be restored? It is no longer good for anything

except to be thrown out and trampled under people's feet. You are the light of the world. A city set on a hill cannot be hidden. Nor do people light a lamp and put it under a basket, but on a stand, and it gives light to all in the house. In the same way, let your light shine before others, so that they may see your good works and give glory to your Father who is in heaven."

Matthew 5:13–16

My good friend Faith Blatchford told me once that relationships are like a bridge for communication. The strength of a relationship determines what type of communication may cross the bridge. As it turns out, standing on the corner and telling sinners they are going to hell has not turned out to be the best form of communication between Christians and nonbelievers. We are called to minister and win souls, and a good way to do that is to focus on meeting people's needs. People rarely open up when they feel condemned or sense that they are a trophy to be won.

Our first goal when engaging lovingly with others should be as a problem solver, not a soul-winner. It echoes a statement I have heard that we are not just ministers in search of souls but supernatural believers looking for problems to solve.

Becoming a problem solver in society is perhaps one of our greatest callings. Jesus said that we are to let our good works shine before men (see Matthew 5:16). Digging down into the original text, we see that *good works* translates as "works, work, career and skills." Knowing this, we see that living a life as followers of Christ means honing our skills and presenting God through our hobbies, talents and gifts. We do not need to preach from the pulpit to reach the lost. Sometimes all we need to do is show our skills and allow the Holy Spirit to do the rest.

The stronger our relational bridges are, the greater our ability is to lovingly confront and to have influence. A husband and wife, for instance, have to be able to communicate openly to one another about their feelings in order for their relationship to work. Children, too, should have an open line of communication that they can use to talk with their parents. Parents should not feel threatened that their children have different opinions than they do. In a healthy family, children learn that their voices matter. Although it may not carry the same voting weight as the parents, it is important they find a place to speak.

I remember several times when our boys complained that we were not parenting them well. My husband would listen and then say, "When you grow up, you can do it your way. Today, this is how we are going to do it."

An example of how the level of a relationship determines the measure of confrontation comes from an experience I had in my church many years ago. A male congregant was giving off creepy vibes of sexual sin. Normally, I would have just prayed and released purity into the atmosphere, but this time, I felt the need to check on him to see what was wrong. I was conflicted on how to approach him, however, since he had not come to me seeking counsel. Because sexual sin can be an uncomfortable topic for a Christian woman to address in a male congregant's life, I asked my husband, Stephen, to do the checking instead.

Not only did Steve already have a greater connection with the man than I did, it was also more appropriate because of the topic they would be discussing. Steve already had spent time building a relational bridge with this congregant, so he was able to talk with him and discover the reason why his personal spiritual broadcast was so sexually charged.

The man confessed to having had a recent struggle with pornography. Stephen, through kindness, walked him toward the healing process of repentance, forgiveness and redemption. Finally, the man prayed and broke free from sexual sin and shame. Through an act of brave communication, Steve was able to cross the relational bridge and help the man confront his struggle.

Therefore confess your sins to each other and pray for each other so that you may be healed. The prayer of a righteous person is powerful and effective.

James 5:16 NIV

If we confess our sins, he is faithful and just and will forgive us our sins and purify us from all unrighteousness.

1 John 1:9 NIV

Whoever conceals their sins does not prosper, but the one who confesses and renounces them finds mercy.

Proverbs 28:13 NIV

In a healthy environment, godly confrontation is a proper step toward a person's freedom. The goal must never be to shame or to lord it over a person, but to approach the situation through love so that you can call him or her up higher.

Advice vs. Control

When my boys were growing up, I fought hard to protect them from making mistakes. But sometimes I had to stand by and allow them to run headlong into the world. As a mom, this was very difficult. Sometimes I knew their ideas would end up in heartache, pain or harm, and it took everything in me to keep from intervening.

Obviously, I did not want them physically harmed, but it was important for me to allow them to learn age-appropriate consequences. Whenever I panicked, my husband would say, "Let them learn, honey. It's a cheap lesson."

"But," I would say, "what happens if they get hurt?"

Stephen would respond, "It's a cheaper lesson now than later. Let them learn this while they are still in our home where we can help them clean up their messes."

It was hard not to control our children, especially when I saw the possible negative outcome of their decisions. Looking back, I have to agree with this age-appropriate leniency. Many adults I know have learned much more from their mistakes than from their successes.

Because the Lord leads me to be a prophetic voice in the world today, I often remind myself of these lessons learned from child rearing. While I am careful to speak any warning I hear from the Lord about what might be coming, it is not my responsibility to control what people do with the information I give. My job is to speak the information. It is the Holy Spirit's job to take it from there.

Christian Boundaries

Another way to make sure we keep love on the shelf is to learn the significance of boundaries. Today many Christians feel they do not have a right to boundaries. When trying to equip themselves with such tools, verses like these are used to counter their efforts: "But I say to you, Do not resist the one who is evil. But if anyone slaps you on the right cheek, turn to him the other also" (Matthew 5:39); "And if anyone forces you to go one mile, go with him two miles" (Matthew 5:41).

For years these verses have been taught as depictions of true Christian love. But they have also been used to dismiss a Christian's right to set healthy boundaries. Christians who are taught they have no right to boundaries fall into the role of becoming *loving enablers*. Although I do believe these verses depict godly love, I do not think they mean that we have to roll over and be walked on. To me, these verses say, "You don't have the power to change who I am. I am in charge of me, not you." If you are interested in pursuing this topic further, the best teaching I have heard on this is in a book called *Keep Your Love On!* by Danny Silk.[1]

In Jesus' day, being slapped was a form of public insult. His command to turn the other cheek is not a call to weak submission, but rather an encouragement to repay evil with good (see 1 Peter 3:9). Jesus wants us to extend grace to those who hate us by responding in kindness: "Repay no one evil for evil, but give thought to do what is honorable in the sight of all" (Romans 12:17); "For the anger of man does not produce the righteousness of God" (James 1:20).

In Genesis, God told Cain, "Sin is crouching at the door. Its desire is contrary to you, but you must rule over it" (Genesis 4:7). I use this verse when explaining how not to agree with the spiritual forces coming against you. The key in any situation is to pause to see as God sees, then partner with Him to release His truth.[2]

I learned the power of these verses firsthand while ministering in Paris during the November 2015 terrorist attack. I was there teaching at a conference when ISIS struck three locations: a restaurant, a stadium and the Bataclan. Many civilians were killed, and I watched as Paris regrouped and grieved with those who had lost loved ones. One of those losses was Helene Muyal-Leiris, who had been the wife of Antoine Leiris. He, a grieving husband and new father, gave a speech to the media about the death of his wife. Below is his heart-wrenching statement:

> On Friday night you stole the life of an exceptional being, the love of my life, the mother of our son, but you won't have my hatred. I don't know who you are and I don't want to know—you are dead souls. If this god for which you kill indiscriminately made us in his own image, every bullet in the body of my wife will have been a wound in his heart.
>
> So no, I don't give you the gift of hating you. You are asking for it but responding to hatred with anger would be giving in to the same ignorance that made you what you are.
>
> You want me to be afraid, to view my fellow countrymen with mistrust, to sacrifice my freedom for security. You have lost. . . .

We are two, my son and I, but we are stronger than all the armies of the world.

I don't have any more time to devote to you. I have to join Melvil who is waking up from his nap. He is barely seventeen months old. He will eat his meals as usual, and then we are going to play as usual, and for his whole life this little boy will threaten you by being happy and free. Because no, you will not have his hatred either.[3]

This is a profound lesson on how to turn the other cheek. Rather than reacting out of hatred or bitterness, this man maintained integrity in the midst of a terrible adversity. That is how the above verses challenge me. They let me know that I am in charge of me. Whenever I feel my emotions or circumstances start to take over, I take a step back and ask the Lord how He sees. Another person's actions cannot change who I am unless I allow them to. As Christians, we must extend grace, bless our enemies and forgive offenses, and when it is needed, set healthy boundaries.

Henry Cloud and John Townsend wrote a wonderful book called *Boundaries: When to Say Yes, How to Say No, to Take Control of Your Life* that I recommend every Christian read.[4] It does a great job of explaining what boundaries are and how to use them properly. Cloud and Townsend argue that boundaries should not be used as weapons against healthy confrontation, but as tools that can help you remove yourself and others from harmful situations. Boundaries are not a form of punishment either, for "perfect love casts out fear" and "fear has to do with punishment" (see 1 John 4:18).

Boundaries are tools we can use to protect ourselves and others. The first step to implementing godly boundaries is to give permission to ourselves to have them.

It is time we asserted healthy boundaries, not only in our personal lives, but also in the world's arena. When we discover a store that has an ungodly policy, we can choose to shop elsewhere. When we are faced with an educational system with a perverted sexual agenda, we can equip our children with truth, remove them from the classroom for that lesson or choose an alternative form of education. Each of these examples is a type of boundary. If you feel victimized by the world's agendas, ask the Holy Spirit what boundaries you can implement to protect yourself and your family.

Even when we use brave communication and healthy boundaries, love still requires sacrifice. Jesus told His disciples, "Greater love has no one than this, that someone lay down his life for his friends" (John 15:13). Sacrificial love will always be a part of the Christian life. Extending grace while being loving is necessary, but remember that we also get to have a voice. We can forgive those who harm us even while enforcing boundaries.

Perhaps one of the greatest purposes for keeping boundaries is to protect our core relationships. Obviously, our most important relationship is with the Lord. With Him, we can process pain, brave storms and move forward into our destinies. Every relationship beyond that flows out of our relationship with Christ.

I experienced the ability to process pain with God firsthand years ago while leading a Sozo session. A man had come to my office to pray with me for his wife's healing. She was fighting stage four cancer and needed a miracle to live. The man had faith that God would intervene, and his faith allowed us to pray through the session and end on a hopeful note. He left my office convinced that his wife would be healed. I, too, felt a sense of growing faith.

Six months later, the man returned. I was excited to hear about his wife's health, so I asked, "How is she?"

"She died," he said.

I froze. Inside, my mind screamed, *He's back to vent his anger at you for not healing his wife!*

I braced myself for an attack, but he stated, "You know, all this time I've been thinking about how God works all things together for good, so I'm here to see what promises He's going to bring out of this."

The man's humility and willingness to forgive left a huge impression on me. Even in the midst of unbearable pain, he was able to take a brave step forward and move closer to God. As I have moved through life, I have recognized that life is messy. Even in times of tragedy, boundaries can be a tool to help protect us. This man's boundary stated, *Nothing can separate me from the love of* God. *Even this will turn out for my good.* Talk about a person keeping his recipe in balance!

Love binds us with the strength we need to get through life's messes. Whenever our needs are not getting met, we can take the issue to God. Love allows us to endure with good boundaries even when we cannot see or imagine the final outcome.

Forgiveness as Self-Love

Forgiveness is one of the greatest tools we can use. I have seen how the enemy twists people's views of forgiveness so that they do not understand the benefit Scripture promises. I often hear the following statements when inviting people to forgive others:

"I just can't forgive him/her. It hurts too much."
"If I forgive them, they will have gotten away with it."
"I won't forgive them, they don't deserve it."

The problem with these reactions is that each is a tactic of the enemy used to bind us to anger, hatred and fear. What we need to remember is that forgiveness is not for the other person's benefit; it is for our own, and forgiveness is one of the most loving things we can do for ourselves.

116

As we repent, God forgives us, and we step out from under the weight of our sin and move into His grace. We become clothed in Jesus' righteousness, which allows us to boldly "draw near to the throne of grace" and cry out, "Abba! Father!" (see Hebrews 4:16; Romans 8:15).

When we release others from bitterness, we acknowledge our own need of forgiveness. We accept God's truth that we must not hide sin, but rather bring it into the light. The benefits of confession and repentance can be astounding: "Therefore, confess your sins to one another and pray for one another, that you may be healed. The prayer of a righteous person has great power as it is working" (James 5:16).

Another benefit of forgiveness is found in the parable of the unmerciful servant:

Then Peter came and said to Him, "Lord, how often shall my brother sin against me and I forgive him? Up to seven times?" Jesus said to him, "I do not say to you, up to seven times, but up to seventy times seven. For this reason the kingdom of heaven may be compared to a king who wished to settle accounts with his slaves. When he had begun to settle them, one who owed him ten thousand talents was brought to him. But since he did not have the means to repay, his lord commanded him to be sold, along with his wife and children and all that he had, and repayment to be made. So the slave fell to the ground and prostrated himself before him, saying, 'Have patience with me and I will repay you everything.' And the lord of that slave felt compassion and released him and forgave him the debt. But that slave went out and found one of his fellow slaves who owed him a hundred denarii; and he seized him and began to choke him, saying, 'Pay back what you owe.' So his fellow slave fell to the ground and began to plead with him, saying, 'Have patience with me and I will repay you.' But he was unwilling and went and threw him in prison until he should pay back what was owed. So when his fellow slaves saw what had happened, they were deeply grieved and came and reported to their lord all that had happened. Then summoning him, his lord said to him, 'You wicked slave, I forgave you all that debt because you pleaded with me. Should you not also have had mercy on your fellow slave, in the same way that I had mercy on you?' And his lord, moved with anger, handed him over to the torturers until he should repay all that was owed him. My heavenly Father will also do the same to you, if each of you does not forgive his brother from your heart."

Matthew 18:21–35 NASB

In these verses, we see how unforgiveness locks us in prison. The king threw the servant who refused to forgive others into jail. So it is with us when we refuse to forgive. These verses are an allegory of how great a rescue God provided us. The master represents God, the servant represents a believer and his fellow debtors are those who harmed him. What we see in this story is how God's grace extends to cover all debts or harm that we have caused Him and others. When we have been forgiven such a great debt, one that took the cross to pay, how can we not also forgive those who owe us?

What I find so useful as a premise of the Sozo ministry is found in verse 35 of Matthew 18. The statement "My heavenly Father will also do the same to you, if each of you does not forgive his brother from your heart" shows us that unforgiveness locks us in prison, where our only escape is to renounce partnership with bitterness.

Many times I have had to encourage people who have been deeply harmed to forgive those who have hurt them, even when they do not feel that they can. I tell them, "I don't have a key to your jail cell—only you and Father God have one. There are only two keys to your prison cell: God's grace and your willingness to forgive."

I find that I often have to help people walk through lesser offenses against them until they are able to forgive greater harms.

I first learned this when a woman I knew came to me for prayer at the urging of a mutual friend. This normally light-hearted lady was not looking happy. She was wearing bitterness openly. When I asked her what was going on, she simply stated that she was ready to leave her husband. According to her, he had changed. He had begun drinking heavily, and she found out that he had betrayed her trust. Upon being discovered, he had repented and started getting help for his alcohol problem, but she had already decided it was too late.

I encouraged her to walk through forgiveness, but her reply was, "I don't want to. He doesn't deserve it."

And here is the problem with the enemy's lie. He tells us that forgiveness should be earned through some form of cleaning up the mess. Yet that is not what Scripture tells us. Forgiveness is not for the other person; it is for us!

As I explained the principles drawn from Matthew 18, she said, "I don't care what the Bible says. I'm not going to forgive him."

Without a way to bring healing, I closed the session, asking her to think about it and return in a couple of days to process her thoughts again.

Two days later, she was back in my office. Her arms were crossed and she had a determined look on her face. She announced, "I won't forgive him, and I'm afraid there is nothing you can say that will change my mind."

I thought, *Oh no, Lord, how are we going to help? I don't have a key to her cell of bitterness.*

Then I heard the Holy Spirit say, *Is there anyone else she can forgive?*

I thought, *Well, let's see.*

I said, "I am not going to force you to forgive your husband, but do you think there is anyone else you would be willing to forgive?"

She stated, "If I do, can I leave?"

119

Knowing the power of forgiveness, I said, "Sure."

She thought for a minute, then threw out these words: "I forgive my co-worker for taking a client away from me. Now I'm done." She stood up and walked out.

Wow, I thought, *I'm not sure that worked very well.*

About a week later she came back to see me one more time, and she seemed a little happier.

I asked, "What happened last week?"

To my surprise she said, "My co-worker and I had the most productive and peaceful week that we've had in years. I think I'm ready to forgive my husband."

And voila! That is the power of forgiveness! Forgiveness does not guarantee the other person will change, but it does release a grace for us to heal from the offenses others have caused. This is why I believe that forgiveness is truly a righteous form of self-love. It unlocks the prison doors and allows us to once again step into the power of God's grace.

DISCUSSION QUESTIONS

1. As a child, did you learn to stay silent or were you allowed to have a voice?

2. Does the concept of relational bridges resonate with you? If so, how?

3. Do you sometimes find that you try to control others? If so, what do you hope to gain from being controlling?

4. Do you have a personal example of turning the other cheek?

5. What did you learn about the Bible verses discussed in this chapter?

6. Were you taught a form of boundaryless love?

7. Is there someone you need to forgive?

ACTIVATION PRAYERS

1. Ask the Holy Spirit whether or not you were allowed to have a voice growing up.
2. Ask Him if there are people in your life with whom you need to set boundaries.
3. Ask the Holy Spirit for wisdom on how to erect and maintain those boundaries.
4. Ask Him if there is anyone you need to forgive.
5. If the answer is yes, ask Him what you need to forgive that person for.
6. Release forgiveness to this person as God directs you.
7. Ask God to forgive you for partnering with bitterness, anger and hatred.
8. Hand Father God all bitterness, anger and hatred and anything else He prompts you to surrender.
9. Ask Him to replace these with love and grace.
10. Ask the Holy Spirit to train you how to walk in true love.

DECLARATIONS

1. I have a powerful voice that I can use gently.
2. I am allowed healthy boundaries and will respect the boundaries others have set with me.
3. I will never again go to bed with unforgiveness in my heart (see Ephesians 4:26).

PART 4

Self-Discipline

Whoever has no rule over his own spirit is like a city broken down, without walls.

Proverbs 25:28 NKJV

8

Substitutes for Self-Discipline

But let him ask in faith, with no doubting, for the one who doubts is like a wave of the sea that is driven and tossed by the wind. For that person must not suppose that he will receive anything from the Lord; he is a double-minded man, unstable in all his ways.

James 1:6–8

When Jesus ministered on earth, He left us some commands to follow. Some of these may seem impossible to fulfill—and without Jesus they truly are—but Christ did not come to earth simply to show us how to live. He came to reveal what life could be like if we partnered with Him:

"But I say to you, Love your enemies and pray for those who persecute you, so that you may be sons of your Father who is in heaven. For he makes his sun rise on the evil and on the good, and sends rain on the just and on the unjust. For if you love those who love you, what reward do you have? Do not even the tax collectors do the same? And if you greet only your brothers, what more are you doing than others? Do not even the Gentiles do the same? You therefore must be perfect, as your heavenly Father is perfect."

Matthew 5:44–48

The word *perfect* in this verse is translated as "brought to its end, finished, mature, and complete."[1] Jesus wants us to be developed fully. To do so, we must master the ingredient of self-discipline.

It is important to clarify the difference between the Greek and Hebrew mindsets when it comes to being "perfect." In the Greek mindset, perfection is attained when there are no flaws. In Hebraic thought, perfection occurs when things are working as designed.

Stephen often illustrates this point by describing an olive tree. To the Greek mind, the olive tree is flawed—it resembles a strange, twisting plant that falls short of being considered beautiful. It is not straight, symmetrical or even impressive in size. To the Hebrew people, however, the tree is perfect because it functions in its ability to produce olives. The Hebrew mindset bases perfection on the subject's ability to function properly, not on its outward appearance.

If something functions as designed, then it is perfect in a Hebrew sense. So when Jesus tells us to be "perfect, as your heavenly Father is perfect" (see Matthew 5:48), He is encouraging us to function as we were designed.

I find that self-discipline is put easily into practice when I have the right mindset. When I work as I am designed by God, it is much easier for me to exercise self-discipline. When I am running in someone else's lane or am wondering in which direction I should go, I find it harder to self-manage.

Self-discipline does not just mean saying no to sin. It is creating a lifestyle that positions us to say yes to God as we

126

pursue His vision for us. One of the easiest ways to remove self-discipline from our shelves is to partner with lies from the enemy that attack our vision and identity.

When we believe lies about ourselves, God and others, we lack the discernment necessary to self-manage. We use substitute spices to make up for our perceived areas of lack. In this chapter, we will examine some substitute spices people apply when their recipes are out of order.

Substitute No. 1—Impatience

Impatience or *hastiness* is defined as "brief, fleeting and superficial" or "impatient and impetuous."[2] The definition implies an inability to trust God's timing regarding a desired outcome or goal. You would be amazed at how many Christians—of all ages—end up in my office because they feel hurt, enraged or disappointed by God. They feel as though they followed what God asked them to do—and they did it in faith!—but now as they wait for His response, heaven's answers seem far away. Because they fear that God will not come through, they take matters into their own hands. It is in this process that the substitute spice of impatience finds an opportunity.

Waiting on the Lord's promises can be difficult, but mastering our immediate desires will allow us to step out from under man's timing to prepare for God's. The goal for any believer is to stay in step with what the Lord is doing and not to move ahead or behind this pace. This might sound easy on the surface, but I have known Christians, myself included, who have spent their entire lives learning to master this principle.

In the Old Testament, Abram and Sarai were promised a son, but they stepped outside of God's timing because of fear that He would not fulfill His promise quickly enough. They devised their own strategy to create an heir:

> Now Sarai, Abram's wife, had borne him no children. She had a female Egyptian servant whose name was Hagar. And Sarai said to Abram, "Behold now, the LORD has prevented me from bearing children. Go in to my servant; it may be that I shall obtain children by her." And Abram listened to the voice of Sarai. So, after Abram had lived ten years in the land of Canaan, Sarai, Abram's wife, took Hagar the Egyptian, her servant, and gave her to Abram her husband as a wife.
>
> Genesis 16:1–3

When we stray from God's plan, sin is the outcome. Abram and Sarai tried to meet their needs apart from God. This led to bad fruit. Although a child was born, he became a symbol of resistance against Abram and his people. I believe this resistance still continues to this day:

> And the angel of the LORD said to her [Hagar], "Behold, you are pregnant and shall bear a son. You shall call his name Ishmael, because the LORD has listened to your affliction. He shall be a wild donkey of a man, his hand against everyone and everyone's hand against him, and he shall dwell over against all his kinsmen."
>
> Genesis 16:11–12

This type of impatience occurred similarly with King Saul. When asked to wait on the prophet Samuel, Saul gave in to fear that God would not act quickly enough, and he performed the sacrifice that Samuel was called to do. The consequence of his inability to wait for Samuel resulted in God removing him from his kingdom:

> Samuel said, "What have you done?" And Saul said, "When I saw that the people were scattering from me, and that you did not come within the days appointed, and that the Philistines had mustered at Michmash, I said, 'Now the Philistines will come down against me at Gilgal, and I have not sought the

favor of the LORD.' So I forced myself, and offered the burnt offering." And Samuel said to Saul, "You have done foolishly. You have not kept the command of the LORD your God, with which he commanded you. For then the LORD would have established your kingdom over Israel forever. But now your kingdom shall not continue. The LORD has sought out a man after his own heart, and the LORD has commanded him to be prince over his people, because you have not kept what the LORD commanded you."

1 Samuel 13:11–14

Saul was unwilling to wait for God's timing, which was in direct disobedience to God. Saul's heart may have been in the right place, but like Abram and Sarai, he failed to trust God completely and acted to make sure his own needs were met.

How often do we give in to the pressure from those around us? It is important that we trust God and restrain from trying to meet our own needs. As we see throughout Scripture, God is eager to take care of us. The goal for us is to trust Him:

Trust in the LORD, and do good; dwell in the land and befriend faithfulness. Delight yourself in the LORD, and he will give you the desires of your heart.

Psalm 37:3–4

Do not be anxious about anything, but in everything by prayer and supplication with thanksgiving let your requests be made known to God. And the peace of God, which surpasses all understanding, will guard your hearts and your minds in Christ Jesus.

Philippians 4:6–7

"O Jerusalem, Jerusalem, the city that kills the prophets and stones those who are sent to it! How often would I have gathered your children together as a hen gathers her brood under

129

her wings, and you were not willing! See, your house is left to you desolate."

Matthew 23:37–38

It is amazing how many Christians say they love God but fail to trust Him. Marriage experts Rob Pascale and Louis H. Primavera, authors of the book *So Happy Together*, say that there is no such thing as love without trust. They write:

> Trust is one of the keystones of any relationship—without it two people cannot be comfortable with each other and the relationship lacks stability. As its basic tenets, trust lets us feel secure because we believe our partner has our back and is loyal through thick and thin. It also allows us to display our thoughts and feelings openly and honestly, because we regard our partner as supportive and don't worry that they will judge, ridicule or reject us. Trust goes hand in hand with commitment: It's only after you feel you can trust someone are you able to truly commit to that person.[3]

Many Christians experience a shallow relationship with the Lord, and a lack of trust is a main reason. The problem, however, is not on God's end. He gave His Son in pursuit of us. The problem originates with us and our lack of trust in Him. If you are aware that you lack trust in God, chances are the substitute spice of impatience is the one you need to work on.

Stephen has a great section on trust in his teaching "Prosperous Soul Foundations." In it he states that faith gets us to believe in God, but trust gets us to apply His Word. When God tells us to give money to a person or to go pray for someone, trust acts as the gasoline to fuel our faith. We carry out instructions from God because we believe that we heard Him, and we trust that He is good.

We need to realize that no Christian can experience a full relationship with the Lord unless trust is at the center. God knows every thought we have, and He numbers the hairs on our heads (see Luke 12:7). If He knows the beginning and end, our presents and futures, how can He not know what we need—and figure out a way to supply it when we need it?

When I feel tempted to step in and take care of my own needs, I remind myself of a simple truth: God is far more interested in me growing up than He is in my comfort. Understandably, this can be a difficult concept to grasp. Many of us long for comfort and push away situations that have the potential to hurt us.

At Bethel we act upon the belief that God is way more interested in building a man than He is a ministry, and therefore, we want to build big people rather than big ministries. When we step in too hastily to take care of ourselves, we miss God's solutions, including any deeper needs He wants to fulfill for us.

Jesus demonstrated patience while being tempted in the wilderness. Although the devil invited Jesus to meet His own needs, Jesus stood firm and pointed out that there were deeper needs that only God could fill:

> And the tempter came and said to him, "If you are the Son of God, command these stones to become loaves of bread." But he answered, "It is written, 'Man shall not live by bread alone, but by every word that comes from the mouth of God.'"
>
> Matthew 4:3–4

We can imagine that after fasting forty days, Jesus was hungry. The devil used this physical need to try to tempt Jesus into performing a miracle to prove His identity: "If you are the Son of God, command these stones to become loaves of bread." Instead of giving in, Jesus refuted the enemy's temptation and pointed out His greater need for spiritual hunger: "Man shall not live by bread alone, but by every word that comes from the mouth of God."

Later, the devil tried to tempt Jesus into testing God's promise of protection: "If you are the Son of God, throw yourself down, for it is written, 'He will command his angels concerning you,' and 'On their hands they will bear you up, lest you strike your foot against a stone'" (Matthew 4:6).

In both of these passages, Jesus understood that there was a deeper need that could only be met through God. I believe the lesson He needed to model for us in this verse was how to lean into faith when trusting God for protection.

When we ask God to protect us, we can be held back by our need to see God perform in an anticipated way. This action might make us miss the next step that we are supposed to take. We must never approach God with expectations of how He will answer or with specific time frames that we require. Quiet trust does not make God prove Himself. It says, *God will protect me the way He wants. What I get to do is follow Him.*

Later, when the devil offered Jesus a shortcut to the throne, Jesus remained strong. He knew His purpose was the cross. Jesus' ability to not take the easier route allowed Him to redeem all of mankind:

> And he said to him, "All these I will give you, if you will fall down and worship me." Then Jesus said to him, "Be gone, Satan! For it is written, 'You shall worship the Lord your God and him only shall you serve.'"
>
> Matthew 4:9–10

If you find yourself being impatient while waiting on a promise from the Lord, ask Him to clarify what your true need is before you rush off to change your circumstances. Allow God to point out if there is a deeper issue that needs to be addressed. Although God provides for all our needs, He wants us to grow up as well (see Philippians 4:19; Hebrews 5:12–14).

Substitute No. 2—Critical Spirit

Believers sometimes partner with a critical spirit but label it as discernment. It comes as a false sense of care that says, "I just want to give you a little advice." A critical spirit also gets expressed as gossip and false concern. "We really need to pray for them since they are struggling so much," becomes a problem when the motive is not truly supporting the person in prayer.

I believe that when true discernment becomes perverted, it finds its voice as a critical spirit. A great first step in keeping this spice out of our recipes is found in Matthew:

> "Why do you see the speck that is in your brother's eye, but do not notice the log that is in your own eye? Or how can you say to your brother, 'Let me take the speck out of your eye,' when there is the log in your own eye? You hypocrite, first take the log out of your own eye, and then you will see clearly to take the speck out of your brother's eye."
>
> Matthew 7:3–5

It is easy to tell when a critical spirit is functioning in other people. Those who partner with it tear others down and complain to anyone who will listen. If you need a current example of a critical spirit, turn on the television and watch the news.

There is another aspect of a critical spirit that should be mentioned. When people partner with a critical spirit and attack themselves, they are joining with what I call *The Punisher*.

I learned this term years ago when I was in a meeting with my mentor, Danny Silk. He was teaching our staff how to create a vision statement and wanted us to write down our perfect day. He began by telling his perfect day, which would start out with sleeping in and getting up leisurely, making pancakes for his kids, wrestling with them a bit, then kissing his wife before heading into his counseling day at work. Once there, he would meet with a couple who had been struggling for years. They would have an epiphany and instantly begin to love each other once again.

When Danny finished, he turned to us and asked, "What is your perfect day?"

I heard my brain shout, *The lame walk, the blind see, the deaf hear and the dead are raised!*

Wow, I thought. *That would be a great day.* Immediately I had another thought.

I can't hang that on my wall. It would bum me out. It would mock me every time I looked at it, reminding me just how few times I have seen this happen.

Not knowing that this was going to be a revealing question, I put my hand up and asked, "Danny, how do you keep your ideal from bumming you out every day?"

I have to admit that the question took him by surprise, and he asked me to clarify my point.

"You know," I said, "like . . ." and I proceeded to tear his perfect day apart line by line.

After a long, shocked pause, he said, "You need to get rid of The Punisher."

The Punisher? I thought, *What's The Punisher? I don't have a punisher. I'm a leader. People love working for me.*

I was stumped. Years earlier I had been delivered of jealousy and a critical spirit. I was no longer the type of person who tore people down. I ran an inner healing ministry that set people free and helped them find their worth.

What Danny's statement revealed was a self-aimed critical spirit with which I had partnered since childhood. It had allowed me to be successful by keeping me out of trouble. I was able to move to the front of the line because I proceeded carefully and did not make missteps. It was quite a revelation to realize that this was not the Holy Spirit, but an internal punisher that prevented me from doing wrong.

I gained freedom when I got rid of this punishing spirit. No longer did the spirit criticize my moment-to-moment actions or keep me awake at night with looped conversations of what I should have said or done differently.

In Sozo sessions when I sense this spirit in others, I have them ask God to show them if they have a measuring stick with which they measure themselves. If they do, I have them ask God what He wants to do with it. Over the years, I have seen many people rejoice as they handed God this ungodly instrument of self-hate.

If you have ever partnered with a critical spirit, repent and ask God for forgiveness. Hand Him The Punisher and ask Him how you can learn to see people the way He does. Then ask for a new revelation of His grace to see yourself the way He sees you.

Substitute No. 3—Double-Mindedness

Fluctuations in faith are common for young believers, but part of the process of growing in maturity means they must move past these seasons of second-guessing. Many Christians lose heart in the midst of their circumstances and as a result lose their faith. Solomon tells us that our ability to stay strong in times of adversity is a measure of our strength: "If you faint in the day of adversity, your strength is small" (Proverbs 24:10).

Most of us want to see God's promises fulfilled quickly. This is not bad; however, maturity means we say yes to His promises no matter how long they seem to be taking. Abraham received the promise that he would be the father of many nations, but it took years for him to produce even one heir. His great-grandson Joseph received a word that his entire family would serve him, but it took almost twenty years before he even made it to Pharaoh's palace. It took even longer for his family to come to Egypt and bow before him.

Most of God's promises take time to be fully realized. This may tempt us to doubt the promises we have received, but God wants us to learn how to stand in the freedom we have gained so that He can move us into deeper healing. We see this process in Exodus:

> "I will not drive them out from before you in one year, lest the land become desolate and the wild beasts multiply against you. Little by little I will drive them out from before you, until you have increased and possess the land."
>
> Exodus 23:29–30

If it seems as if God is tarrying, it is likely that He has already spoken and is waiting for you to finish His last command. Many times I have heard Bill Johnson say that if you have stopped hearing God, go back to the last time you heard Him and obey whatever it was that He told you to do.

When we walk in spiritual maturity, we use self-discipline on a regular basis. It keeps us tied to God's timing and promises. In contrast, double-mindedness is a tool the enemy uses to keep us questioning our beliefs.

You can always tell the presence of double-mindedness because it asks questions like, *Did God really say?* This familiar question strays dangerously close to the serpent's prompt in the Garden. When Lucifer questioned Eve, his first and primary form of attack was getting her to question God's command: "Now the serpent was more crafty than any other beast of the field that the LORD God had made. He said to the woman, 'Did God actually say, "You shall not eat of any tree in the garden"?'" (Genesis 3:1).

When you feel double-mindedness whistling through your head, take time to step back and be alert. It could be the enemy's voice. Satan and his armies thrive on doubt, and the Bible says those who doubt should not expect anything from God:

> But if any of you lacks wisdom, let him ask of God, who gives to all generously and without reproach, and it will be given to him. But he must ask in faith without any doubting, for the one who doubts is like the surf of the sea, driven and tossed by the wind. For that man ought not to expect that he will receive anything from the Lord.
>
> James 1:5–7 NASB

The Bible tells us that faith pleases God (see Hebrews 11:6). Double-mindedness does the opposite. It erodes our ability to stand on what God has said. If you struggle with double-mindedness, repent and ask God for forgiveness. Take some time to reflect on the words He has spoken. Go back to when you were convinced you heard Him and ask Him how you should proceed.

Double-mindedness also manifests when we have a conflict in our moral compass. When we do not keep our eyes fixed on Jesus, the Author and Finisher of our faith, we can get pulled from the narrow path that God has asked us to walk. This type of double-mindedness starts with entertaining incongruent thoughts and opens a door to denial and delusion.

Substitute No. 4—Denial

There are three types of denial with which we can partner: (1) a denial of God's Word as the whole truth; (2) a denial of the reality in which we find ourselves; and (3) a denial of the battle that we as believers are in. When we deny God's Word as truth, we open a door that leads to full-blown delusion. Denial can be as simple as believing the lie that God does not really care about our sin, or as complex as starting a cult because someone believes he or she is a god.

Denial of God's Word

The first type of denial begins when a seed of justification gets planted in your heart. It sounds like, "If God is truly loving, He wouldn't want me to stay in this boring marriage." Another example is, "Homosexuality isn't a sin. If it was, I wouldn't be struggling with it."

When you find yourself overlooking Scripture in the Bible, you have already opened yourself to delusion. Denying the truth of God's Word is a dangerous first step in skewing your ability to keep a sound mind. Here is a sobering excerpt from Romans about denial's slippery hold:

> For the wrath of God is revealed from heaven against all ungodliness and unrighteousness of men who suppress the truth in unrighteousness, because that which is known about God is evident within them; for God made it evident to them. For since the creation of the world His invisible attributes, His eternal power and divine nature, have been clearly seen, being understood through what has been made, so that they are without excuse. For even though they knew God, they did not honor Him as God or give thanks, but they became futile in their speculations, and their foolish heart was darkened.
>
> Romans 1:18–21 NASB

In this passage, we see how not honoring God slides into a complete fall from morality: "And although they know the ordinance of God, that those who practice such things are worthy of death, they not only do the same, but also give hearty approval to those who practice them" (Romans 1:32 NASB). Denial of God's Word as truth always leads us away from a sound mind.

Partnering with denial gives us permission to transfer our sin onto other people. Denial allows us to believe that others are the cause of our problems. This happened with a man I found myself ministering to years ago. He was thinking of leaving his wife. He and another woman had already begun an emotional affair, and they wanted to take it to a physical level. The church leaders scheduled a last-minute session for him with me in hopes that he would see the role that denial was playing in his relationship with his mistress. The more we talked, the more he kept justifying his desires.

"You don't know what I've had to deal with," he said. "My wife is ruining my life. It's only fair that I get to do what I want."

His descent into self-pity made it impossible to carry on an honest conversation. He was in complete denial of his own shortcomings. No matter how well I presented the issues, he refused to see how any of his marital problems were his fault. We ended the session without any progress. Sadly, he was unwilling to see the wrong in his actions, and he refused to move toward repentance. Denial of his sin became full-blown delusion.

Denial of Reality

The second form of denial happens when people fail to face reality. This is seen in people who are too afraid to ask hard questions like, "God, where were You when I was little and needed protection?" It can create a life based on false logic. If you never allow yourself to ask God difficult questions, then you will be forced to come up with your own flawed answers. This is not to say that other believers and the study of God's Word cannot bring wisdom. My point is that God has answers for all of our heartache.

Sometimes it is as simple as, "You know what? I don't need to know the answer. I'll just trust You, God, and see what good comes from this."

There were multiple times in my life when I lost someone very dear and special to me. In one case, my family and I prayed earnestly for healing. We called Bethel's intercessor team and had every friend and family member contending for a miracle. Our family member's healing never came, and it forced me into a quiet time of heated discussion with the Lord.

I believe it is important that we vent our frustrations with the Lord. As we embrace our positions as adopted sons/daughters and friends of God, it is up to us to create an atmosphere of transparency. The Lord knows our thoughts, so we might as well voice them and see what He says. Sometimes He will not say anything. Sometimes all He wants to do is listen.

For those of you who have experienced heartbreak and tragedy, I encourage you to set some time aside with the Lord and ask Him, "God, where were You?" Be sure to allow His truth into the situation. Try to stay away from anger or justification. If you ask for His truth, He will show you:

> My God, my God, why have you forsaken me? Why are you so far from saving me, from the words of my groaning? O my God, I cry by day, but you do not answer, and by night, but I find no rest.
>
> Psalm 22:1–2

> "Oh that my vexation were weighed, and all my calamity laid in the balances! For then it would be heavier than the sand of the sea; therefore my words have been rash. For the arrows of the Almighty are in me; my spirit drinks their poison; the terrors of God are arrayed against me."
>
> Job 6:2–4

> And about the ninth hour Jesus cried out with a loud voice, saying, "Eli, Eli, lema sabachthani?" that is, "My God, my God, why have you forsaken me?"
>
> Matthew 27:46

Some of these verses above might seem harsh or even hopeless, but if we look further, we see that each dark moment was met with a turn toward hope:

And we know that for those who love God all things work together for good, for those who are called according to his purpose.

Romans 8:28

Yet you are holy, enthroned on the praises of Israel. In you our fathers trusted; they trusted, and you delivered them.

Psalm 22:3–4

Then Job answered the LORD and said: "I know that you can do all things, and that no purpose of yours can be thwarted. 'Who is this that hides counsel without knowledge?' Therefore I have uttered what I did not understand, things too wonderful for me, which I did not know."

Job 42:1–3

When Jesus had received the sour wine, he said, "It is finished," and he bowed his head and gave up his spirit.

John 19:30

I want to take this moment to encourage you to go to Father God, Jesus and the Holy Spirit. Unload your most difficult questions and invite His peace into your situation. I promise that truth will be given. Not all of your questions will be answered the way you expect, but if you listen with an open heart, you will find peace.[4]

Denial of Warfare

When it comes to the substitute spice of denial, the third problem I see is that Christians sometimes deny the warfare that is going on around them. It is as if they have stuck their heads in the ground. They fail to see the enemy's fiery arrows flying at them. They refuse to look realistically at the situations

141

in which they find themselves. This is most noticeable when people come in for financial Sozo sessions. They do not see that they have created a problem. Usually these problems surface through symptoms like overspending, credit card debt or lavishness.

As I teach "Shifting Atmospheres" around the world, I encounter many who have partnered with denial. This partnership creates a false sense of safety. Scripture makes it clear that we are in a war: "For our struggle is not against flesh and blood, but against the rulers, against the powers, against the world forces of this darkness, against the spiritual forces of wickedness in the heavenly places" (Ephesians 6:12 NASB).

Denying that the spiritual realm exists is dangerous. If you do not understand where attacks are coming from, you will assign motives to other people and circumstances. This can lead to fighting with people instead of the true enemy.

One step further on the denial trail leads us to blame God when our lives fall apart. Usually this happens when people experience a tragic event and fail to receive an answer to the question *Why didn't He protect me?* We blame God for His lack of protection rather than acknowledge the fact that the enemy, not God, is the one causing the trouble:

> Let no one say when he is tempted, "I am being tempted by God," for God cannot be tempted with evil, and he himself tempts no one. But each person is tempted when he is lured and enticed by his own desire. Then desire when it has conceived gives birth to sin, and sin when it is fully grown brings forth death. Do not be deceived, my beloved brothers.
>
> James 1:13–16

> In the beginning was the Word, and the Word was with God, and the Word was God. He was in the beginning with God. All things were made through him, and without him was not any thing made that was made. In him was life, and the life was the

light of men. The light shines in the darkness, and the darkness has not overcome it.

John 1:1–5

Of all the substitute spices for self-discipline that can clutter our shelves, denial is perhaps the most damaging. A major deception from the enemy, it rewrites a person's understanding of his or her situation so that all that is seen is confusion. This explains how some influential church leaders rise in their ministries one day and fall morally the next. They deny that they have weaknesses or that they need "lesser" people to hold them accountable.

Do not be deceived. We are in a war. We must take up our shields of faith and not delusion or denial. If you are wrestling with a plan that God did not provide but you think there is no other way but to follow it through, then you are already walking in denial of His ability to turn all to good (see Romans 8:28). You may even be sliding toward delusion.

If you feel like delusion is influencing your life, then I call you back to your senses in Jesus' name! I command your mind to clear and your senses to reignite. I invite the Holy Spirit to seek you out and engage your spirit so that delusion fails to be your endgame. I ask Jesus by His grace to release wisdom over your life in place of denial and delusion.

GROUP DISCUSSION QUESTIONS

1. Do any of the examples in this chapter resonate with you? If so, which ones?

2. What are ways that the enemy has been tempting you to lose your self-control?

3. Is there a way God has been prompting you to maintain self-discipline?

ACTIVATION PRAYERS

1. Ask the Holy Spirit if you have been partnering with impatience.
2. If so, ask Him to forgive you for partnering with it.
3. Ask the Holy Spirit if you have been struggling with double-mindedness.
4. If so, ask Him to forgive you for not trusting His plan for your life.
5. Ask the Holy Spirit if you have partnered with a critical spirit.
6. If so, ask Him to forgive you for partnering with it.
7. Hand Him all agreements you have made with a critical spirit and ask Him what He wants to give you in exchange.
8. Ask the Holy Spirit if you have been partnering with denial, fantasy or delusion.
9. If so, repent for any way you have been viewing your circumstances through powerlessness or self-pity.

DECLARATIONS

1. I have the mind of Christ (see 1 Corinthians 2:16).
2. My weapons of warfare are powerful for the tearing down of strongholds (see 2 Corinthians 10:4).
3. I can do all things through Christ who strengthens me (see Philippians 4:13).

9

Keeping Self-Discipline
on the Shelf

When you sit down to eat with a ruler, observe carefully what is before you, and put a knife to your throat if you are given to appetite.

Proverbs 23:1–2

Self-discipline is a very important ingredient for our recipes. A person who walks in power but lacks self-discipline will transmit a message of "Me, me, me!" and walk in entitlement—demanding his or her needs to be met. A person who walks in love but lacks self-discipline will fail at setting healthy boundaries. Both of these ingredients—power and love—are essential, but self-discipline is what keeps them in a healthy balance.

Self-discipline is "the ability to control one's feelings and overcome one's weaknesses."[1] A lack of self-discipline is what led to mankind's need for Jesus in the first place. After creation, God gave Adam and Eve one rule, "of the tree of the knowledge of good and evil you shall not eat" (see Genesis 2:17). With the rest of the Garden to enjoy, one might think this command would be easy to follow. But when Adam and Eve were tempted, they were unable to honor God's expected boundary. Why? Because they lacked self-discipline.

Self-discipline is our ability to toe the line when other options call out to us. It holds us in check even when more fun or easier alternatives are presented. When Jesus was tempted by Satan in the desert, several easier options were presented (see Matthew 4:1–11). One was turning a stone into bread for nourishment. Another was bowing down to Satan in exchange for humanity. I am sure each of these tests would have been easy for Jesus to give in to. Thankfully, He knew to follow God's commands instead. His success in doing so showed His skill with self-discipline.

This is why it is important for us to renew our minds. In Joyce Meyer's book *Battlefield of the Mind*, she exposes how critical it is for us to take ownership over our thoughts:

> The mind is the leader or forerunner of all actions. Romans 8:5 makes it clear: "For those who are according to the flesh and are controlled by its unholy desires set their minds on and pursue those things which gratify the flesh, but those who are according to the Spirit and are controlled by the desires of the Spirit set their minds on and seek those things which gratify the [Holy] Spirit."
>
> Our actions are a direct result of our thoughts. If we have a negative mind, we will have a negative life. If, on the other hand, we renew our mind according to God's Word, we will, as Romans 12:2 promises, prove out in our experience "the good and acceptable and perfect will of God" for our lives.[2]

Our goal as Christians should be to focus on truths that gratify the Spirit. These truths include love, joy, peace, patience, kindness, goodness, faithfulness, gentleness and self-control (see Galatians 5:22–23). It is interesting to note how self-control (nearly identical to self-discipline) makes it on the list.

Other truths that can help us renew our minds include possessing the mind of Christ and seeing reality the way God sees it (see 1 Corinthians 2:16; 1 Samuel 16:7). When we partner with each of these truths and allow them to take hold, then maintaining self-discipline is much easier.

Christ spoke often about the importance of self-discipline, and He warned what would happen if we failed to discipline our thoughts:

> "You have heard that it was said, 'You shall not commit adultery.' But I say to you that everyone who looks at a woman with lustful intent has already committed adultery with her in his heart."
>
> Matthew 5:27–28

> "You have heard that it was said to those of old, 'You shall not murder; and whoever murders will be liable to judgment.' But I say to you that everyone who is angry with his brother will be liable to judgment; whoever insults his brother will be liable to the council; and whoever says, 'You fool!' will be liable to the hell of fire."
>
> Matthew 5:21–22

In these verses, Jesus reveals that God holds our thoughts to a high standard. It is not enough to appear righteous; we must also *be* righteous. Jesus also exposes how our inner beliefs slip out into our daily realities:

> "The good man out of the good treasure of his heart brings forth what is good; and the evil man out of the evil treasure brings forth what is evil; for his mouth speaks from that which fills his heart."
>
> Luke 6:45 NASB

Our inner thoughts lead to outward manifestations. If we take care to monitor our inner lives, then our outer lives will follow. This is what Paul highlighted in 2 Corinthians:

> For the weapons of our warfare are not of the flesh but have divine power to destroy strongholds. We destroy arguments and every lofty opinion raised against the knowledge of God, and take every thought captive to obey Christ, being ready to punish every disobedience, when your obedience is complete.
>
> 2 Corinthians 10:4–6

Though thoughts are a physical component of our brains, Paul says our weapons are not of the flesh. I have found that the supernatural power to break habits and sinful patterns starts when we first dismantle unhealthy spiritual mindsets.

Hooks of the Enemy

If we are going to walk in self-discipline, we must first dislodge the enemy's hooks in our lives. *Enemy hooks* are weak points or vulnerabilities the devil can exploit. They are similar to the concept of *open doors*, where a person's unresolved sin attracts demonic influence. These hooks are attached to lies we believe about ourselves, others or God.

If, for example, someone believes the lie that he or she is worthless, a hook of worthlessness will develop. That person will begin to filter comments from others through the lens of *I am worthless*. Unless we take these thoughts captive and replace the lies about ourselves, others or God, we will remain raw and vulnerable to mindsets that pull us from our place of peace. Hooks can form from any lies we believe about ourselves, others or God. You can tell when you are believing a lie because it pulls you further from truth.

Lies can be self-targeted, like "I'm stupid" or "I'm ugly"; they can be aimed at others, such as "If I were rich like Bill Gates, I'd be happy"; or they can even be targeted at the Lord, like "God doesn't hear my prayers" or "God doesn't care about me." We must learn to discern the lies we believe and remove their influence, so that any hooks or open doors we carry will be destroyed.

Hooks are tricky and will continue to pop up until the lie that supports them is removed. Remember when I talked about my son who struggled with suicide? It was not until he broke agreement with the catastrophic spirit that he was able to break free once and for all. In order to break agreement with the catastrophic spirit (hook), we needed to find the lie attached to it. The lie Cory believed was, *Life's too difficult. Why not take the easy way out?* The hook that supported this lie was the spirit of catastrophe.

People believe all sorts of lies, and these lies create hooks in us that the enemy can use to bait us. I remember years ago when a young, attractive woman came in for a Sozo session. She confessed to comparing herself to others. She was pursuing acting in the entertainment industry and had a huge calling on her life, yet she found herself discouraged because she compared her looks, talent and career with others.

Once she and I discovered the lie that she was not good enough, we located the hook of worthlessness and removed its control. The session ended with her encountering Jesus. His truth that she was beautiful and perfect according to His design allowed her to leave my office with a greater understanding of her self-worth. To this day, she walks in a greater measure of self-confidence that has manifested positively in her career.

The key to breakthrough with lies, hooks and open doors is learning how to exchange ungodly mindsets for truth. One of the best ways we can do this is through reading God's Word.

Nothing works better to uproot lies and expose truth than Scripture. Consider these words from Solomon:

My son, be attentive to my words; incline your ear to my sayings. Let them not escape from your sight; keep them within your heart. For they are life to those who find them, and healing to all their flesh. Keep your heart with all vigilance, for from it flow the springs of life. Put away from you crooked speech, and put devious talk far from you. Let your eyes look directly forward, and your gaze be straight before you. Ponder the path of your feet; then all your ways will be sure. Do not swerve to the right or to the left; turn your foot away from evil.

Proverbs 4:20–27

It is interesting to see how following God's Word brings life and lasting health. As Christians, we should be poring through Scripture and using it as a primary weapon against the enemy:

For the word of God is living and active, sharper than any two-edged sword, piercing to the division of soul and of spirit, of joints and of marrow, and discerning the thoughts and intentions of the heart.

Hebrews 4:12

And take the helmet of salvation, and the sword of the Spirit, which is the word of God.

Ephesians 6:17

But he answered, "It is written, 'Man shall not live by bread alone, but by every word that comes from the mouth of God.'"

Matthew 4:4

But he said, "Blessed rather are those who hear the word of God and keep it!"

Luke 11:28

The Word implanted in our minds and hearts helps us to discern right from wrong. Understanding God's guidelines helps us to watch over our hearts and brings us to a higher level of accountability and self-discipline.

I hear people complain that the Bible is too restrictive. I do not see the Bible as restrictive; rather, I see it as a map that I can follow to make sure I do not end up taking a wrong path. The above verses give us a key for how we can guard our hearts and put away all forms of deceit. By keeping our gazes ahead, we can make sure our feet follow the correct path:

> Blessed is the man who walks not in the counsel of the wicked, nor stands in the way of sinners, nor sits in the seat of scoffers; but his delight is in the law of the LORD, and on his law he meditates day and night. He is like a tree planted by streams of water that yields its fruit in its season, and its leaf does not wither. In all that he does, he prospers.
>
> Psalm 1:1–3

It is important that we allow the Bible to speak to us so that when people give us counsel that contradicts truth, we will be able to instantly discern their advice as false. In a world that has become averse to absolutes, we must remember that God's Word is truth. It is not watered down or out of fashion. We must keep it close to our hearts if we are going to engage self-discipline and be trees planted by streams of water.

Stewarding Self-Discipline

Another aspect of walking accurately in this world is to develop a personal relationship with the Holy Spirit. He is our Helper, our Comforter and our Teacher. Without Him, it is impossible to walk uprightly. Here are some verses that reflect this truth:

Or do you not know that your body is a temple of the Holy Spirit within you, whom you have from God? You are not your own.

1 Corinthians 6:19

"But the Helper, the Holy Spirit, whom the Father will send in my name, he will teach you all things and bring to your remembrance all that I have said to you."

John 14:26

"But you will receive power when the Holy Spirit has come upon you; and you shall be My witnesses both in Jerusalem, and in all Judea and Samaria, and even to the remotest part of the earth."

Acts 1:8 NASB

And the disciples were continually filled with joy and with the Holy Spirit.

Acts 13:52 NASB

For the kingdom of God is not eating and drinking, but righteousness and peace and joy in the Holy Spirit.

Romans 14:17 NASB

Now may the God of hope fill you with all joy and peace in believing, so that you will abound in hope by the power of the Holy Spirit.

Romans 15:13 NASB

Guard, through the Holy Spirit who dwells in us, the treasure which has been entrusted to you.

2 Timothy 1:14 NASB

It is our connection to the Holy Spirit that enables us to discern the enemy's attacks. With His insight, we can prepare ourselves for battle, gain insight and release His power into our situations.

Cultivating an intimate relationship with the Holy Spirit may seem difficult, but the more you practice, the easier it gets. It is possible to learn how to pay attention to His promptings, sense His presence and follow His lead.

Although most of us have been encouraged to talk to God, few of us have been trained to listen when He responds. Many times we take for granted that it is the Holy Spirit who nudges us to *Ask her if she is okay. Take that extra sandwich to work. Pray for him. Take a left here.* When we begin to follow the Holy Spirit's promptings, we begin to experience divine encounters.

How many times have you had an impression but ignored it? Maybe you felt encouraged to take an item from your house to work but you talked yourself out of it—only to find out later that you really needed it! Maybe you have had moments in your car when you felt like you needed to slow down or change lanes only to find out seconds later that the traffic in front of you was stopping unexpectedly. Have you been prompted to pray for someone but remained silent because you were afraid of how silly it would make you look?

One such prompting occurred to me while I was visiting friends in the United Kingdom. I was riding down in the elevator to meet them when a well-dressed woman got on and joined my ride.

As soon as she got on, I thought, *Wow, she looks really great in her outfit.* I smiled to myself and continued riding down when I felt a nudge from the Holy Spirit. *Dawna, tell her how nice she looks.*

I really did not want to bother her and seem like a pushy American, but the need to compliment her kept getting stronger. Finally, I looked at her and said, "I'm sorry to bother you, but I am an American and I just wanted to let you know how smart you look in that suit."

Immediately she relaxed, smiled and said, "Thank you so much. I was standing in front of the mirror wondering if I had picked the right outfit for the day. You see, in about thirty minutes, I am going to be standing up in front of a bunch of people reading off the election results, and I want to look my best."

Wow, I thought, *the Holy Spirit is so kind to give that woman a gentle hug before she gets up in front of everyone.*

This type of story happens to me often, and I hope it encourages you. As you cultivate your relationship with the Holy Spirit, you will enjoy the payoffs for each risk you take in following His promptings.

Accountability

Accountability is another tool we can use to help us grow in self-discipline. It is important that we allow others to speak into our lives so they can "spur [us] on toward love and good deeds" (Hebrews 10:24 NIV). It is vital that we connect with other believers who are further along in their walk with Christ. They have wisdom to share that can keep us from having to learn through the school of hard knocks.

When I was a young mom, I made sure that I surrounded myself with other moms and grandmothers in a weekly women's study. Not only did it give me the ability to have my son play with other preschool kids, but it helped me to draw upon the wisdom of the other moms.

After watching my son's behavior in a particular setting, one of the grandmas told me, "It will be okay. He will grow out of it."

I remember thinking, *She has no idea what I am dealing with.* But guess what? She was right.

I love the following verse. It has kept me going to church, even in times when I wanted to stay home:

> And let us consider how to stimulate one another to love and
> good deeds, not forsaking our own assembling together, as is

the habit of some, but encouraging one another; and all the more as you see the day drawing near.

Hebrews 10:24–25 NASB

If we are just attending Sunday services to go through the motions because we think it makes us look like good Christians, or we attend simply to put a check mark on our calendar of attendance, we may miss out on important personal interactions. It is important that we invite people into our circles who can talk us through concerns and share in our struggles. "As iron sharpens iron, so one person sharpens another" (Proverbs 27:17 NIV).

Others can see from a perspective that is outside of our pressures and concerns. They can filter our circumstances through their own life lessons to see our situations from another angle. Many times I have processed difficult situations with friends and have come away with new ideas about how to handle them. Other times, I have gained the courage needed to move forward steadily.

If you are not already in a small group or weekly Bible study, I would urge you to find one. Encouraging others and being empowered by friends are important aspects of a healthy Christian walk.

Power of Saying No

It is hard sometimes to stand up against the world's opinions and say no. The world may fight back and accuse you of being narrow-minded or a bigot. But it is important to understand truth and to fight for it, even when other options are being presented.

> We know that our old self was crucified with him in order that the body of sin might be brought to nothing, so that we would no longer be enslaved to sin. For one who has died has been set free from sin.
>
> Romans 6:6–7

We are meant to look and act differently than the world. We are not meant to blend in:

> "You are the salt of the earth; but if the salt has become taste-less, how can it be made salty again? It is no longer good for anything, except to be thrown out and trampled under foot by men. You are the light of the world. A city set on a hill cannot be hidden; nor does anyone light a lamp and put it under a basket, but on the lampstand, and it gives light to all who are in the house."
>
> Matthew 5:13–15 NASB

Throughout my life I have had to remind myself that I need to look different from the world. That fact influences my deci-sions. It may mean not accepting invitations to certain events, or if I do choose to attend, carrying myself in a godly manner while I am there. While attending university, my son was invited to many important poetry reading after-parties. He felt a need to mingle with his colleagues, so he attended them.

One night, an important poet-colleague looked at him and said, "Cory, something about you is different. What is it?"

Before Cory could answer, someone else piped up and ex-claimed, "It's Jesus, dude!"

Our *no* can be powerful in helping us both to maintain self-discipline and to allow our lights to shine before men.

Obedience

An important aspect in maintaining self-discipline is wielding the weapon of obedience. When my appetites scream at me to give in, I declare, "I am a child of obedience, and I will not partner with this sin." This phrase has walked me through many precarious situations where my desires failed to match up with my godly character.

Sometimes freedom with God is instantaneous. You enter a prayer session feeling one way and then leave a few hours later feeling the exact opposite. I love these moments. I also realize, however, that sometimes healing requires hard work and takes time. Many times I have seen God remove old lies supernaturally and then impart His truth to people, but they still have to walk out their freedom from the learned mindsets.

When you feel set free from a hook or sinful habit in your life but still desire it, remember that it takes about 21 days to change a habit. While choosing your new truth, you will need to partner continually with obedience. This is when I really ground myself in God's Word, and I make sure I understand what God is desiring for me.

Years ago, after realizing I was partnering with a spirit of fantasy, I broke agreement with its hold. It still took time before I was able to turn off its baiting voice. I expected my deliverance to be both instantaneous and lasting. As I began walking out my freedom, however, I realized that my gravitation to this spirit was attached to a deeper need. As long as I felt loved and cared for by others, I was able to ignore this spirit's allure. But on days where I did not feel appreciated, I found it hard to escape the spirit's pull toward false significance. This was especially hard after a tough day when I was tired and less resistant to the lure of this spirit.

Many nights I would shed tears as I told this voice, "I am a child of obedience, and I will not go away with you tonight." Much like Sy Rogers who would tell God, "I want to do this (sin), but I am choosing to do this (non-sin) instead," it was a stance of obedience that silenced these ungodly thoughts.

If you are in a situation now where it is hard to renounce sin, I encourage you to make a stand for righteousness. Be honest with God and invite the Holy Spirit to speak to you as you stand in obedience to His Word.

GROUP DISCUSSION QUESTIONS

1. What areas in your life need an increase in self-discipline?

2. How much time do you spend in God's Word?

3. How strong is your personal connection with the Holy Spirit?

4. Are there safe people in your life who can hold you accountable?

5. Where in your life are you standing obediently against some desire?

ACTIVATION PRAYERS

1. Ask the Holy Spirit if you need an upgrade in self-discipline.

2. If the Holy Spirit says yes, ask Him:

   a. If He wants you to read the Bible more.

   b. If He wants you to spend more time with Him.

   c. If He wants you to find a weekly study group.

   d. If He wants you to stand in obedience against an ungodly desire with which you have been struggling.

3. Write down what the Holy Spirit tells you.

4. Tell a friend or accountability partner what the Holy Spirit tells you and give them permission to check on you weekly to see how well you are stewarding this revelation.

DECLARATIONS

1. I am a light to this world (see Matthew 5:14).
2. I take all ungodly thoughts captive (see 2 Corinthians 10:5).
3. I am a child of obedience and will not partner with sinful desires any more.
4. He who has been set free is free indeed (see John 8:36).

PART 5

Application

"Everyone then who hears these words of mine and does them will be like a wise man who built his house on the rock. And the rain fell, and the floods came, and the winds blew and beat on that house, but it did not fall, because it had been founded on the rock."

Matthew 7:24–25

10

Living a Fear-Free Life

Therefore, my beloved brothers, be steadfast, im-
movable, always abounding in the work of the Lord,
knowing that in the Lord your labor is not in vain.

1 Corinthians 15:58

We have spent the last nine chapters learning God's plan for overcoming fear. Now it is time to apply it. Here are some practical steps we can take to identify fears in our lives and remove their influence.

Discovery is the first step to breaking free from fear. This requires partnership with the Holy Spirit, and it begins by asking, "Holy Spirit, are there any lies I am believing?"

If the Holy Spirit answers yes, then ask, "Holy Spirit, what are they?"

Once the Holy Spirit tells you the specific lie, do a simple prayer of renunciation. An example of this looks like, "Holy Spirit, thank You for showing me this lie (insert whatever lie He showed you). I hand it to You in Jesus' name."

163

After we have given up the lie, an exchange should happen. Exchanging the enemy's lies for truth is one of the most important steps in the healing process. In fact, I might even say it is the most important.

The process is as simple as asking, "Holy Spirit, what's the truth?"

When I pray with people, I make sure they always hear from God about His truth. I do this because if the space where a lie once occupied is left unfilled, the enemy may come back later and put another lie in its place (see Matthew 12:45).

In Sozo sessions, people tend to follow this formula—and it works wonders. Though it is not a cure-all, I have seen it yield incredible fruit. If you are having trouble identifying or dealing with fear, consider partnering with the Holy Spirit and following these three steps: discovery, renunciation and exchange.

The reason I go over these steps is because I believe in the importance of getting healthy. Examining bad fruit in our lives allows us to come close to God and to receive His healing. Jesus said, "A healthy tree cannot bear bad fruit, nor can a diseased tree bear good fruit" (Matthew 7:18). If there is unhealthy fruit in our lives, we need to bring it to Jesus so He can prune it.

Knowing our *tells/cues* helps us understand when we find ourselves moving toward unhealthy coping mechanisms (an act of bad fruit). When these unhealthy actions occur, we know that our formula is off-balance. Bad fruit (behaviors) being produced tends to signify that we have bad roots (beliefs) that need to be removed. Giving these beliefs to Jesus brings about the restoration we desperately need.

The Orphan Mindset

Months ago I met Carl and his wife, Linda, at a Sozo seminar. Although he gave off the sense of being a gentle man, his wife had a fragile and abused look. If I was discerning correctly, there was a secret family issue that needed to be broken off for them both to walk free.

I have found that fear is usually a response people use when they feel powerless or unprotected. This tends to come from an orphan mindset that says, "You are alone. No one else cares about you." When people partner with an orphan mindset, they tend to bristle up. This is usually because their beliefs of "I am abandoned" and "I am alone" cause them to activate their inner defenses. People may try to puff up bigger by partnering with anger to appease this sense of insignificance or lack of value.

Keep in mind that an orphan mentality does not mean a person is actually an orphan. Plenty of children with loving biological parents grow up believing that they are unloved, unwanted or abandoned. Being a spiritual orphan has nothing to do with your biological parents. It, instead, deals with the spiritual mindsets that you believe.

It is important to note that there are two types of orphans: those with false spices of power (bullies) and those who partner with powerlessness (victims). Powerful orphans or bullies partner typically with self-reliance, performance and fear of failure. They believe that no one is going to take care of them, so they bully others into submission to feel safe. A powerless orphan sees life as always happening to him or her. Usually this takes the form of a victim mindset.

In Carl and Linda's case, I was pretty sure an orphan mindset was present. Although they presented themselves as a peaceful, loving couple, I anticipated that they were partnering with a bully and a victim mindset.

I asked Carl what he wanted to work on in our Sozo session. Without blinking he said, "Anger."

I had already spotted the effect of this on their marriage, but I played innocent and asked, "How does anger manifest in your life?"

"We have been Christians for over ten years. When I surrendered to God, Jesus came in and changed my heart. But every so often, I find myself erupting with rage even though I know it is not how God wants me to respond."

Aha! I thought. *This explains the terror-stricken look on his wife's face.*

Although they had been Christians for years, Linda still anticipated that her husband would act harshly. His frequent outbursts kept her from feeling confident that he would maintain his self-control in future situations.

We prayed and asked the Lord to take Carl to the first time he had partnered with rage. Carl told me God was showing him a memory from when he was eight years old. As he told me, his body stiffened.

I asked, "What's going on?"

"Every summer I used to stay with my grandma. Whenever I did something wrong, she would beat me with a two-by-four."

Really? I thought. "Can you ask Jesus where He was during this memory?"

Carl prayed and said, "I see Jesus standing at my side taking the worst hits."

At this point Carl began to weep.

"All this time," he said, "I've wondered why she never broke any of my ribs. Now I know it's because Jesus took the worst of it."

"What does this truth mean for you?" I asked.

"That I'm not alone," Carl said. "I don't need rage to make me feel big. I'm not that trapped eight-year-old boy on the porch anymore."

In this session, Carl broke off the lie that he was alone, which was the first step in removing the orphan spirit with which he had partnered. Having partnered with the orphan spirit left him feeling powerless and small, and he acted out from that sensation with rage. Once Carl dismantled the triggering belief that he was unloved and alone, he was able to see himself as a fully grown man capable of protecting himself.

Honesty—with God and Man

On the surface, people who close off rather than explode seem more peaceful than their counterparts; however, their inner reality can be the opposite. This is what happened with a young woman, Alys, who came in to see me for a Sozo session.

Alys was a new believer who was struggling with years of physical pain. Throughout our session, all her answers about God were, "I know He loves me. We're best friends. We're so good." Her answers sounded healthy, but I could tell something was off. I felt she was avoiding the real issues underneath the surface.

No matter what questions I asked, she always injected her answer with a very spiritual response, saying things like, "Everything's okay. I just know that God is great."

I asked, "How does your husband feel about you always being in pain?"

"I don't know," she said. "We don't talk about it."

"Can you ask Jesus why that is?"

"I guess," Alys said.

I waited a few moments and then leaned forward. "Can you hear, see or sense anything?"

"Jesus told me that I'm afraid my husband is going to lecture me. I'm afraid that if I tell my husband about my pain, he'll just lecture me on how I need to take better care of myself. He's always telling me to slow down and rest."

Interesting, I thought, mulling this over.

Alys was using her spiritual connection with God to hide from her husband's lecturing. She was afraid to experience his perceived lack of care in her pain. Her avoidance of communicating with her husband fueled her attempt to deny any pain she was experiencing.

I asked Alys to repent for having used avoidance as a way to protect herself. Once she did, she was able to forgive her husband for not being gentle, and she broke agreement with her fear of his harshness.

My session with Alys taught me that it is always important to remain honest with God and man. It never helps to hide due to fear of interpersonal conflict. Remember, fear is never our friend. When we bring avoidance of others into our relationship with God, we skew our understanding of the answers He gives.

Bad Fruit

As you walk out your freedom, try not to ignore any spices you have stocked on your shelf. Instead, honestly look at your ingredients. Take inventory of what you have placed inside your metaphorical kitchen. If there are unhealthy spices or ungodly substitutes, remove their influence by bringing them into the light. Anything the devil throws at you can only survive by being left in the dark. Confession and repentance are some of our greatest tools for healing:

> Therefore confess your sins to each other and pray for each other so that you may be healed. The prayer of a righteous person is powerful and effective.
>
> James 5:16 NIV

> If we confess our sins, he is faithful and just and will forgive us our sins and purify us from all unrighteousness.
>
> 1 John 1:9 NIV

> Whoever conceals their sins does not prosper, but the one who confesses and renounces them finds mercy.
>
> Proverbs 28:13 NIV

"Repent, then, and turn to God, so that your sins may be wiped out, that times of refreshing may come from the Lord."

Acts 3:19 NIV

When we hide our sins (or bad fruit) in darkness, they thrive. When we expose them to light, they are uprooted quickly. These sins and spices can only survive when we refuse to take them to Jesus. The Bible warns:

"Likewise, every good tree bears good fruit, but a bad tree bears bad fruit. A good tree cannot bear bad fruit, and a bad tree cannot bear good fruit. Every tree that does not bear good fruit is cut down and thrown into the fire. Thus, by their fruit you will recognize them."

Matthew 7:17–20 NIV

Jesus' words should be an encouragement for us, not a source of fear. When we recognize bad behavior in ourselves, we need to confront it head-on. If you notice a sin or an ungodly spice, seek the Holy Spirit. Ask Him why you are producing bad fruit, and have Him show you the belief system that is producing it.

In my own life, a major telltale sign of bad fruit is when I feel the need to defend myself. I can feel myself bristle up and stand taller. I have learned in these moments to calm myself down so that I do not step into sin.

I do not consider this practice in and of itself freedom. I would call this the beginning steps of self-control. True freedom would be removing the root from the tree that is causing the bad fruit. How I deal with such situations is simple. I find somewhere quiet and ask God, "What just happened there? What was I feeling that made me want to self-protect? What lie am I believing?" In all my years of using this process, I have always heard an answer. It may not have come right away, but pressing in with God always reveals truth.

After I pray and receive God's perspective on these events, I renounce the lies that have influenced my thoughts or actions. I forgive the person who I thought was threatening me and move on. This is what freedom looks like—taking every opportunity to examine the heart's fruit and giving it to God.

God's Perspective

A key component of my fear-removing strategy is to stop and ask God for His perspective on the situation. It never ceases to amaze me how differently He sees. It reminds me of the story when the angel of the Lord told Gideon (who was hiding in a winepress), "The LORD is with you, O mighty man of valor" (Judges 6:12).

Gideon's choice to hide from his enemies does not seem mighty or valiant. But God rarely looks at the outward appearance (see 1 Samuel 16:7). When God sees us, He calls out the gold that is hidden within. He calls forth the treasure He has placed inside of us.

If you struggle with powerlessness or insignificance, take some time to find out what the Lord thinks about you. Stop right now and ask Him some questions. Tell him how you feel. Ask Him where you learned the lies that you believe. Ask Him to impart the truth about how He sees you.

When we know God's perspective, it gives us the courage to start walking out our freedom. When life's naysayers speak about how they see us, we can partner with God and discard their false assessments. When we know how God sees us, we can walk in confidence of who we are and work to become more like Christ.

Growing up I enjoyed sports more than dolls. My mom was athletic, and she hated makeup and dresses. Naturally, I followed in her footsteps. At the age of five, I was enrolled in a martial arts class. I continued working at that skill until I was well into my teens. Needless to say, I carried a high preference of athleticism over beauty.

Fast forward twenty years and I was now in my adulthood—a wife with a husband and two kids. I was hungry to hear God's voice. I often waited in the prayer lines at church to get a word from Him, and I begged God to give me a small picture or vision. I remember the day I finally received that picture from Him.

I saw a big hand with a seed that looked like an emerald. Somehow I knew the hand was Father God's and that the small emerald seed was me. As I contemplated this picture, I heard the Lord say, *"Look at what I have created. Isn't she beautiful?"*

It has been thirty years, and I still have not forgotten this image that affirmed my identity. From that moment on, I began to buy makeup, dresses and other girly accessories. I still enjoy playing sports, but I also look forward to dressing up and giving the other gals a run for their money. As I type this, I am smiling at my blue fingernail polish that features a little flower on one nail.

When God spoke His truth to me, it dispelled all the lies that I had believed about myself. When He said, "Isn't *she* beautiful?" it dispelled any gender myths about me being too boyish or having the wrong likes. Because of God's truth, I was allowed to step into who He truly made me to be.

Discernment

One of the most frequent weapons I use when combating lies is the gift of discernment. I believe that it is one of the most powerful and yet most unused gifts in the body today. Because discernment can be seen as a "taste test" that allows us to see if our recipes are out of balance, all believers should apply it to make sure what they are hearing is truth. The Bible places great importance on it:

> And it is my prayer that your love may abound more and more, with knowledge and all discernment, so that you may approve what is excellent, and so be pure and blameless for the day of Christ.
>
> Philippians 1:9–10

> But solid food is for the mature, for those who have their powers of discernment trained by constant practice to distinguish good from evil.
>
> Hebrews 5:14

> Beloved, do not believe every spirit, but test the spirits to see whether they are from God, for many false prophets have gone out into the world.
>
> 1 John 4:1

Discernment is our ability to distinguish spirits, and it is a core tenet of the Church that should be practiced daily. Without it, we can fail to distinguish between truth and error and may end up walking on the wrong path.

I cannot tell you how many times I have been saved from deception just by stepping aside and asking the Lord to confirm His voice. We receive a lot of thoughts in our brain—some experts claim it is upwards of fifty thousand per day.[1] If we take the time to step back and ask the Lord if a thought, feeling or impression is His, we will receive His guidance to clarify which way we should go.

If you ever find yourself confused, ask God to give you His gift of discernment. We should also read the Bible, as His Word is our ultimate source for truth:

By this you know the Spirit of God: every spirit that confesses that Jesus Christ has come in the flesh is from God, and every spirit that does not confess Jesus is not from God. This is the spirit of the antichrist, which you heard was coming and now is in the world already.

1 John 4:2–3

Seizing Freedom

One last tool I will again highlight is the finding of your *tells*. These are hints or signs your body, spirit or emotions are giving you that something is wrong. If you get really good at identifying them, you can see easily when you are acting beneath your godly character.

If people, for example, who are normally cheerful start to feel grouchy or rage-filled for no apparent reason, chances are their bodies, spirits or emotions are telling them something is off. They are feeling scared, stressed or worn-out.

I know my older son gets grouchy when he does not have an adequate day of rest. He is a strong introvert and needs plenty of time alone in order to recharge. One of Cory's *tells* is when he starts to get cranky. If there is no obvious reason that he can identify for this shift in mood, then he knows it is time to get alone and take a break.

Demonic forces can also influence our spirits and emotions. If you feel uncertain about where a particular feeling is coming from, you can always find a quiet spot and ask God. If the feeling, thought or emotion you are experiencing is coming from the enemy, you can always pray for God's protection and command it to go away.

Once you identify your *tells*, you can partner with Holy Spirit to see what fruit is growing in your heart. After you identify the lies you are believing, exchange them for God's truth and thank Him for His goodness. If you practice this, you will walk in a greater measure of freedom.

Take care to renew your mind every time negative talk comes your way. It will allow you to create new, healthy pathways in your brain. The more truths you embrace, the easier freedom will be to navigate.

Before I close, allow me to leave you with one more verse. It is one of my favorites, and it reminds me every day to keep the right ingredients on the shelf. May your fear-free life always be plentiful:

> Finally, brothers, whatever is true, whatever is honorable, whatever is just, whatever is pure, whatever is lovely, whatever is commendable, if there is any excellence, if there is anything worthy of praise, think about these things.
>
> Philippians 4:8

GROUP DISCUSSION QUESTIONS

1. What bad fruit do you see growing from your tree?
2. Where do you think this unhealthy habit or bad fruit comes from?
3. Do you still have a go-to spice or tool that you use when feeling fear?
4. Do you know what God says about you?

ACTIVATION PRAYERS

1. Ask the Holy Spirit if there are any lies you still believe about yourself.
2. Ask Him where they came from.

3. Forgive anyone who taught you this lie.

4. Ask the Holy Spirit to show you His truth in exchange for this lie.

5. Ask Him if there are any lies you believe about someone else.

6. If so, ask Him to show you the truth about this person.

7. Hand the Holy Spirit any colored lenses you currently see this person through.

8. Ask the Holy Spirit to give you His vision so that you can see this person anew.

9. Ask the Holy Spirit if there are any lies you believe about God.

10. If so, ask the Holy Spirit where you first learned this lie.

11. Forgive whoever taught you this lie as truth.

12. Hand to the Holy Spirit any lies you have believed about God, then ask Him to exchange them for truth.

13. Ask Father God, "What do You think of me?" and write it down.

14. Ask Jesus, "What do You think of me?" and write it down.

15. Ask the Holy Spirit, "What do You think of me?" and write it down.

DECLARATIONS

1. I am a new creation in Christ (see 2 Corinthians 5:17).

2. I can do all things through Christ who gives me strength (see Philippians 4:13).

3. I am conforming to the image of Christ (see Romans 8:29).

4. Every day I become more like Him (see Romans 12:1–2).

5. Fear is not my friend; I partner with the mind of Christ (see 1 Corinthians 2:16).

Closing Thoughts

What Now?

Congratulations! You have started your lifelong journey toward fear-free living. I would like to share one last word of advice before you go: Do not be discouraged if you encounter resistance from the enemy in your areas of victory. The demonic forces will oftentimes attack in areas of breakthrough to make it seem like you never got free.

If this happens to you, do not worry. The devil loves to cast doubt and make us think we never experienced freedom in the first place. If such an attack occurs, confront it head-on and declare, "I see you, discouragement (or whatever the enemy is throwing at you), and I am not partnering with you. I send you back in Jesus' name."

If you do not feel an immediate shift toward peace, repeat this prayer until you do. Work through the three steps we discussed in the previous chapter: identification, renunciation and exchange. See if the Holy Spirit reveals any lies that you are believing. I promise, working hard at this will yield incredible results.

I hope you have enjoyed studying the keys to freedom found in this book. I pray that through practice you begin to live fearlessly and see the enemy's strongholds crumble in your life.

Remember, because of Christ's sacrifice, you are no longer a slave to fear. Thanks to the cross, you are now an adopted son or daughter of God. Everything you need has already been paid for. All you have to do is ask:

> "Ask, and it will be given to you; seek, and you will find; knock, and it will be opened to you. For everyone who asks receives, and the one who seeks finds, and to the one who knocks it will be opened."
>
> Matthew 7:7–8

> If any of you lacks wisdom, let him ask God, who gives generously to all without reproach, and it will be given him. But let him ask in faith, with no doubting, for the one who doubts is like a wave of the sea that is driven and tossed by the wind. For that person must not suppose that he will receive anything from the Lord; he is a double-minded man, unstable in all his ways.
>
> James 1:5–8

> "Or which one of you, if his son asks him for bread, will give him a stone? Or if he asks for a fish, will give him a serpent? If you then, who are evil, know how to give good gifts to your children, how much more will your Father who is in heaven give good things to those who ask him!"
>
> Matthew 7:9–11

> It is the glory of God to conceal things, but the glory of kings is to search things out.
>
> Proverbs 25:2

Glossary

Throughout this book, I have used a wide variety of terms that we employ frequently within the Sozo ministry. In my attempt to be clear, I have created a list of words and personal definitions to help you understand what a word means when I use it. These definitions are not definitive, in most cases they are not from a dictionary and they do not represent every usage of a word. If you run into a term within this book that you are not clear about the way in which I am using it, this is a resource to which you can turn.

A

Absolutes: the standard of right and wrong based on the ultimate authority (God) outside of the temporal definition of one person or a group of people.

Abundant Life: a life lived in fullness; a believer experiencing the reality of Christ's presence and peace on an ongoing basis.

Abuse: harm inflicted on another human being, can be physical or emotional; a form of control.

Anxiety: a lack of peace.

B

Belief System: a collection of thoughts or convictions that make up a larger moral code.

Boundary: a defined physical or emotional line intended to protect one's own self and others from perceived harm.

Boundaryless Love: the practice of not being able to set healthy boundaries with others.

Brave Communication: the practice of communicating needs to others in a healthy and respectful way.

Breakthrough: a sudden increase in anointing, knowledge or understanding.

C

Catastrophic Spirit: a demonic spirit that tricks people into partnering with chaos. People who partner with catastrophe tend to see problems as hopeless.

Colored Lenses: lenses that tint the way life is seen. Such lenses result from partnering with skewed perspectives, and these viewpoints tend to develop in childhood and are usually based on a lie.

Critical Spirit: an evil spirit that urges people to judge others.

Culture of Honor: a belief system that encourages others to value one another, especially leaders.

D

Deception: a result of believing lies from the enemy.

Deliverance: freedom from demonic strongholds in a person's life.

Delusion: an inability to face reality, a final step in the deception process.

Demonic Attachments: areas that give access to the enemy; can be a lie, wound or unresolved sin.

Demonic Mindsets: perspectives or thought patterns that align themselves with evil; anything that takes us further away from God.

Denial: a failure to admit that something is real; one of the first steps in the deception process.

Discernment: the quality of being able to comprehend or perceive the spiritual realm.

E

Enablers: people whose refusal to confront allows others to remain in their dysfunction.

Enemy: dark or negative forces; Satan.

Entitlement: a mindset that makes people feel that they are owed a specific answer or outcome.

Exchange: when giving a lie to God, Jesus or the Holy Spirit, a truth is given in return; trading a lie for a truth.

F

Faith: dependence, belief.

Fantasy Spirit: a spirit that tricks people into escaping into an alternate reality.

Father God: our Creator; the first Person of the Godhead.

Father Ladder: a tool the Sozo ministry uses to help clarify the connections between lies that have been learned from childhood and the relationships formed with each member of the Godhead.

Father Wound: a wound or issue involving a painful event or memory regarding a father figure.

Fear: a lack of trust in God; expectation of harm or failure.

Fear Door: the first and most frequently encountered of the Four Doors. Inside this door is found worry, unbelief, need for control, anxiety, isolation, apathy, drugs and alcohol addictions.

Fear of Lack: the worry of not having enough.

Forgiveness: the result of being forgiven or forgiving; to stop blaming others for pain and suffering; to stop requiring payment from another.

Four Doors: a tool the Sozo ministry uses to identify strongholds in a person's life.

G

Generational Spirit: a sin learned from parents or grandparents, or a demonic attachment that has followed down through the family line.

Godhead: another word for the Trinity; the Father, Son and Holy Spirit.

God's Word: the holy and inspired Word of God; a Christian's source for truth.

H

Hindrance: a negative mindset or demonic attachment that makes the act of connecting with God difficult.

Holy Spirit: God's Spirit; a source for comfort and instruction.

Hooks: areas the enemy uses for exploitation; a weakness or lie the enemy can exploit.

I

Identity: one of the primary needs Father God provides. The character or traits that distinguish who a person is.

Impatience: the inability to wait peacefully; unwillingness to depend on God's promises when they are not fulfilled right away.

Inner Healing: the practice of dealing with emotional hurts or pains of the heart in an attempt to bring peace and health.

Irrational Fear: fear that holds no basis in reality; typically, a fear from the enemy.

J

Jesus: God's Son; our Savior. Our source of daily communication and companionship.

Jezebel Spirit: a demonic spirit of control that can attach to a human in order to control and dominate others; can masquerade as a victim.

K

Kingdom: eternal worldview; heaven on earth; God's dominion on earth as it is in heaven.

L

Lie: an untrue or inaccurate statement. A common tactic of the enemy.

Love: an unconditional and affectionate concern for the good of another; one of three ingredients used to combat fear (see 2 Timothy 1:7).

M

Mammon: wealth personified; money deified; greed and avarice; a demonic spirit that controls thoughts toward and use of money.

Manipulation: an evil form of control over a person to serve one's own self-interests.

Mother Wound: a wound that resides in a past pain or memory involving a mother figure.

O

Orphan Spirit: a demonic mindset that is steeped in powerlessness and abandonment.

P

Panic Attack: a sudden overwhelming feeling of acute and disabling anxiety which involves a physical manifestation of fear; usually tied to some deeper need.[1]

Paradigm: mindset or viewpoint.

Parental Panic: instantaneous and overwhelming fear of harm for a child.

Passive-Aggressive: communicating one's needs in a manipulative fashion.

Perfection: in the Hebrew mindset, perfection simply means functioning as designed; the Western world tends to view perfection in terms of flawlessness.

Perseverance: the ability to hold true to a predetermined course.

Phobia: an extreme or irrational fear of or aversion to something.[2]

Predatory Spirit: a demonic spirit or mindset that tricks people into hurting or desiring to hurt others.

Presenting Jesus: a Sozo tool used to find where lies originate in a person's life.

Protection: preventing injury; one of the needs Father God provides.

Provision: supplies being available when needed.

Power: physical, emotional or spiritual strength; one of three ingredients used to combat fear (see 2 Timothy 1:7).

Powerlessness: a lack of physical, emotional or spiritual strength.

Poverty Mindset: an attitude steeped in lack.

The Punisher: a critical spirit that punishes people either internally (toward self) or externally (toward others).

R

Renounce: refusing to recognize or submit to a harmful or destructive mindset.

Root/Root System: where a lie begins.

S

Self-Discipline: the practice of controlling one's thoughts and actions; one of three ingredients used to combat fear (see 2 Timothy 1:7).

Self-Protective Pattern: a recurring strategy people use to protect themselves from others.

Self-Satisfaction: the practice of meeting one's own needs.

Self-Sufficiency: dependence on self rather than God.

Seven Mountains of Society: a teaching made popular by Lance Wall-nau; the idea that there are seven realms (or mountains) that influence the development of society.

Shifting Atmospheres: a teaching that helps people identify the negative spirits being broadcast over a region, place or person; this information can be used to see what the enemy is doing so that the Church can partner with God to see what He wants to impart in its place.

Sibling Wound: a wound caused by a painful past event involving a sibling or close friend.

Silent Treatment: a form of manipulation used to punish others by remaining silent.

Sinful Pattern: a recurring pattern of sin that has a foothold on someone's life.

Soul: a person's mind, will and emotions.

Sozo Ministry: an inner healing and deliverance ministry aimed at discovering the root issues blocking personal connection with God.

Spirit: the essence of a person that is eternal, remaining after the death of the physical body; it is with the spirit that one believes unto salvation.

Spirit of Invisibility: a demonic spirit that partners with insignificance and being unseen.

Spirit of Suicide: a demonic spirit that tricks people into partnering with severe hopelessness that results in people taking their own lives.

Spiritual Atmosphere: the spiritual reality, mindset or message that is hovering over a person, place or region; can be good or bad.

Spiritual Broadcast: a message or mindset that the enemy is sending over a person, place or region.

Spiritual Realm: the unseen, nonmaterial world that is thought either to influence or precipitate change in the physical world.

Stress: a state of mental or emotional strain or tension resulting from adverse or demanding circumstances.[3]

Strongholds: spiritual or emotional obstacles and hindrances that restrain people from walking in complete freedom.

Substitutes/Spices: practices or lies to which people turn in order to feel powerful, loved or in control.

Superiority: considering oneself to be of more importance than others.

T

Toxic Thoughts: lies or unhealthy mindsets.

Transformation Center: the main campus for the Sozo and Shabar ministries in Redding, California.

Traumatic Events: experiences that cause deep harm and lasting wounding.

Trinity: the Father, Son and Holy Spirit.

Truth: the accurate Word of God.

U

Unforgiveness: an unwillingness to release someone for an offense or a wound; this act of holding resentment leads to bitterness and demonic harassment.

Unhealthy/Ungodly Mindset: an inaccurate thought process or wrong belief that pulls individuals further from the truth.

Unresolved Wounds: hurts and pains from the past that have yet to be healed; these become places of weakness the enemy and others can exploit.

V

Victimization: the practice of either harming or hurting another human being; stealing someone's power.

Victim Mindset: the belief that one stands alone against a hostile world; a feeling of powerlessness against life's circumstances.

W

Worry: anxious or troubled about actual or potential problems.[4]

Notes

Introduction

1. Sozo is an inner healing ministry that works to strengthen people's connections with each member of the Trinity (Father, Son and Holy Spirit). By identifying lies about God, themselves or others, people are empowered to reject ungodly influences and move on with embracing God's truth. Once clients accept God's truth, they can then move on to pursue wholeness without the prior self-sabotage they had been experiencing. You can find out more about Sozo in my first book that I co-authored with Teresa Liebscher, *Sozo: Saved, Healed, Delivered: A Journey into Freedom with the Father, Son, and Holy Spirit* (Shippensburg, Pa.: Destiny Image, 2016).

2. *Dictionary.com*, s.v. "abundantly," accessed October 10, 2017, http://www.dictionary.com/browse/abundantly?s=t.

Chapter 1: The Problem with Fear

1. "Impact of Fear and Anxiety," *Taking Charge of your Health & Well-being*, accessed March 6, 2018, https://www.takingcharge.csh.umn.edu/enhance-your-wellbeing/security/facing-fear/impact-fear.

2. Katherine Weber, "Rick Warren: Why God Encourages Christians to 'Fear Not' 365 Times in the Bible," *Christian Post*, April 30, 2016, http://www.christianpost.com/news/rick-warren-why-god-encourages-christians-to-fear-not-365-times-in-the-bible-163029/.

Chapter 2: The Recipe Revealed

1. "11 Facts About Anxiety," DoSomething.org, https://www.dosomething.org/us/facts/11-facts-about-anxiety.

2. Sigmund Freud, *A General Introduction to Psychoanalysis*, trans. by G. Stanley Hall (New York: Boni and Liveright, 1920), Bartleby.com, 2010, http://www.bartleby.com/283/25.html.

3. Caroline Leaf, *Switch On Your Brain: The Key to Peak Happiness, Thinking, and Health* (Grand Rapids, Mich.: Baker Books, 2015).

Chapter 3: Why Power Gets Removed from the Shelf

1. Dawna De Silva, *Shifting Atmospheres: Discerning and Displacing the Spiritual Forces around You* (Shippensburg, Pa.: Destiny Image, 2017).

Chapter 4: Powerless Substitutes

1. "Porn Addiction Stats—Pornography Addiction Statistics, Percentages, Numbers, & Info," *Tech Addiction*, accessed September 8, 2017, http://www.techaddiction.ca/pornography-addiction-statistics.html.

2. Peg Streep, "What Porn Does to Intimacy: 3 studies find that explicit material can do more harm than most people think," *Psychology Today*, July 16, 2014, https://www.psychologytoday.com/us/blog/tech-support/201407/what-porn-does-intimacy.

3. The question is in reference to the three times Peter was asked if he was a follower of Christ (see Luke 22:54–62).

4. Christopher Ingraham, "Nearly 1 in 10 Americans Have Severe Anger Issues and Access to Guns," *Washington Post*, April 8, 2015, https://www.washingtonpost.com/news/wonk/wp/2015/04/08/nearly-1-in-10-americans-have-severe-anger-issues-and-access-to-guns/?utm_term=.86b34b414bd7.

5. "Mental and Substance Use Disorders," Substance Abuse and Mental Health Services Administration, updated September 20, 2017, https://www.samhsa.gov/disorders.

6. "Statistics on Drug Addiction," American Addiction Centers, accessed October 12, 2017, https://americanaddictioncenters.org/rehab-guide/addiction-statistics/.

7. "Understanding Drug Use and Addiction," National Institute on Drug Abuse: Advancing Addiction Science, last modified June 2018, accessed February 4, 2018, https://www.drugabuse.gov/publications/drugfacts/understanding-drug-use-addiction.

8. Two wonderful books by Yvonne are *Dancing on the Graves of Your Past* (Charleston: CreateSpace, 2009) and *Trauma, Sexual Exploitation, and Addictive Self-Harm with Keys to Healing* (Charleston: CreateSpace, 2015).

9. Interview with Sy Rogers, https://nicolepartridge.com/wp-content/uploads/2011/05/Alive-Dec07-Jan08-Pge-26-28-Sy-Rogers.pdf.

Chapter 5: Powerfully Alive

1. Stephen K. De Silva, *Prosperous Soul Stewardship Series: Foundations Manual* (Redding, Calif.: Accent Digital Publishing, Inc, 2010).

2. "Lance Wallnau Explains The Seven Mountains Mandate," YouTube video, 00:43, posted by "Bruce Wilson," July 16, 2009, https://www.youtube.com/watch?v=qQbGnJd9poc.

3. Danny Silk, *The Culture of Honor: Sustaining a Supernatural Environment* (Shippensburg, Pa.: Destiny Image, 2009).

Chapter 6: What's Love Got to Do with It?

1. "Bill Johnson—Sex and the Body (2017 Sermon)," YouTube video, posted by "Kingdom Emissary," July 17, 2017, https://www.youtube.com/watch?v=GI XJZvBG_MA.

2. Stephen addresses this topic of Mammon in his manual *Prosperous Soul Stewardship Series: Foundations*, as well as his online course, which you can register for on https://stephenkdesilva.com.

Chapter 7: Keeping Love on the Shelf

1. Danny Silk. *Keep Your Love On!: Connection, Communication and Boundaries* (Redding, Calif.: Red Arrow Publishing, 2013).

2. For more information on this idea, check out my book *Shifting Atmospheres*.

3. Emily Kent Smith, "'Our one-year-old son will insult you with his happiness and freedom every day': Father's defiant message to ISIS after his wife was killed in Bataclan terror attack," *Daily Mail*, November 17, 2015, www.dailymail .co.uk/new/article-3322348.

4. Henry Cloud and John Sims Townsend, *Boundaries: When to Say Yes, How to Say No, to Take Control of Your Life* (London: Strand Publishing, 1996).

Chapter 8: Substitutes for Self-Discipline

1. *Blue Letter Bible*, s.v. "perfect," accessed June 12, 2017, https://www.blue letterbible.org/lang/lexicon/lexicon.cfm?Strongs=G5046&t=ESV.

2. *Dictionary.com*, s.v. "hastiness," accessed August 10, 2017, http://www.diction ary.com/browse/hastiness?s=t.

3. Rob Pascale and Louis H. Primavera, "Do You Trust Your Partner?", *Psychology Today*, May 19, 2017, https://www.psychologytoday.com/us/blog/so -happy-together/201705/do-you-trust-your-partner.

4. For more on how to process a hard season with God, check out Teresa Liebscher's book *The Book of Healing: A Journey to Inner Healing Through the Book of Job* (Shippensburg, Pa.: Destiny Image, 2018).

Chapter 9: Keeping Self-Discipline on the Shelf

1. *English Oxford Living Dictionary*, s.v. "self-discipline," accessed August 5, 2017, https://en.oxforddictionaries.com/definition/self-discipline.

2. Joyce Meyer, *Battlefield of the Mind: Winning the Battle in Your Mind* (New York: Warner Books, 2002), 3–4.

Chapter 10: Living a Fear-Free Life

1. Neuroskeptic, "The 70,000 Thoughts Per Day Myth?," *Discover: Science for the Curious* (blog), May 9, 2012, http://blogs.discovermagazine.com/neuroskeptic /2012/05/09/the-70000-thoughts-per-day-myth/#.Wz1cZiOZM0o.

Glossary

1. *English Oxford Living Dictionary*, s.v. "panic attack," accessed July 1, 2018, https://en.oxforddictionaries.com/definition/panic_attack.

2. *English Oxford Living Dictionary*, s.v. "phobia," accessed July 3, 2018, https://en.oxforddictionaries.com/definition/phobia.

3. *English Oxford Living Dictionary*, s.v. "stress," accessed July 3, 2018, https://en.oxforddictionaries.com/definition/stress.

4. *English Oxford Living Dictionary*, s.v. "worry," accessed July 3, 2018, https://en.oxforddictionaries.com/definition/worry.

After a radical encounter with the Holy Spirit more than twenty years ago, a passion for both individual and corporate freedom was released into **Dawna De Silva's** heart. Following the lead of Jesus and oversight of Beni Johnson at Bethel Church in Redding, California, Dawna founded the International Bethel Sozo Ministry that she still co-leads with Teresa Liebscher.

As well as authoring several bestselling books, Dawna is an internationally sought-after speaker who releases freedom to the Body of Christ wherever she goes. Whether it is teaching on God's promise of abundant life or partnering with Jesus for the healing for the body, soul and spirit, Dawna's passion is to see all believers walk fully in the destiny God has for them.

Dawna lives in Redding with her husband, Stephen, also an international speaker and author. They have two sons, Cory and Tim, and two amazing daughters-in-law.

Most of the tools listed in this book have been used for years in the Sozo ministry. If at any point you feel compelled to investigate them further, consider checking out Dawna and Teresa Liebscher's book *Sozo: Saved, Healed, Delivered.*

If you wish to find out more about De Silva Ministries, visit www.dawnadesilva.com. If you want information about Bethel Sozo or are interested in scheduling a Sozo session with an approved minister, visit www.bethelsozo.com. If you want to find a nearby Sozo team, information is available on the website under the "Sozo Network" and "Regional Facilitators" tabs.